FATTY LIVER DIET COOKBOOK

2000 Days of Quick, Easy, and Delicious Recipes to Cook for Health–Including a Step-by-Step Guide and 28–Day Meal Plan to Detoxify, Cleanse, and Boost Energy

Disclaimer

The information provided in this cookbook is for educational and informational purposes only and is not intended as health or medical advice. The recipes and suggestions in this book are not a substitute for professional medical advice, diagnosis, or treatment. Always seek the advice of your physician or other qualified health provider with any questions you may have regarding a medical condition or dietary concerns.

The author and publisher disclaim any liability for any adverse effects or consequences arising from the use or application of the information contained in this book. The reader is solely responsible for their health and safety when following the recipes and advice in this book.

While every effort has been made to ensure the accuracy and completeness of the information, the author and publisher make no guarantees or warranties of any kind, express or implied, regarding the use or results of the information provided in this book.

Nicole Cobb

2024

TABLE OF CONTENTS

CHAPTER 4: Lunch

CHAPTER 5: Dinner

CHAPTER 6: Light Snacks and Appetizers

CHAPTER 7: Vegetable

CHAPTER 8: Healthy Desserts

CHAPTER 9: Smoothies

CHAPTER 10: Beverages for Liver - Cleansing

CHAPTER 11:

INTRODUCTION

Welcome to the Fatty Liver Diet Cookbook, your comprehensive guide to nourishing your body while supporting liver health. Whether you have been diagnosed with fatty liver disease or are simply looking to improve your liver function, this cookbook is designed to provide you with delicious and healthful recipes that are easy to prepare and enjoyable to eat.

What You'll Find in This Cookbook

This cookbook is designed to make following a fatty liver diet enjoyable and sustainable. Here's what you can expect:

Delicious Recipes: With over 200 recipes, this cookbook offers a diverse range of options that are both liver-friendly and flavorful. Whether you prefer hearty breakfasts, satisfying lunches, delectable dinners, or guilt-free desserts, there's something for everyone to enjoy while meeting their dietary needs.

Nutritional Guidance: Each recipe includes detailed nutritional information to help you make informed choices about what you're eating. You'll also find tips on ingredient substitutions and modifications to accommodate different dietary preferences and restrictions.

Meal Planning Tips: We're not just here to provide recipes, we're here to support you throughout your dietary journey. Our cookbook offers practical advice on how to plan and prepare meals that support liver health, from stocking a liver-friendly pantry to making meal prep easier.

What is Fatty Liver Disease?

Fatty liver disease, also known as hepatic steatosis, is a condition characterized by the accumulation of ex
cess fat in the liver. It can be broadly categorized into two types: non-alcoholic fatty liver disease (NAFLD) and alcoholic fatty liver disease (AFLD). Understanding these conditions is crucial as they can lead to more serious liver problems if not managed properly.

Non-Alcoholic Fatty Liver Disease (NAFLD)
NAFLD is the most common form of fatty liver disease, particularly in Western countries. It occurs in individuals who drink little to no alcohol. NAFLD is often associated with obesity, insulin resistance, type 2 diabetes, and metabolic syndrome. There are two main stages of NAFLD:

Simple Fatty Liver (Steatosis): This is the early stage where fat accumulates in the liver cells but does not cause significant inflammation or liver damage.

Non-Alcoholic Steatohepatitis (NASH): This more severe stage involves liver inflammation and damage, which can progress to fibrosis (scarring), cirrhosis (severe scarring), and liver cancer.

Alcoholic Fatty Liver Disease (AFLD)
AFLD results from excessive alcohol consumption, which damages the liver and leads to fat accumula-

tion. The severity of AFLD can vary based on the amount and duration of alcohol intake. Like NAF-LD, AFLD can progress through stages:

Alcoholic Steatosis: Early stage characterized by fat accumulation in the liver.

Alcoholic Hepatitis: Involves inflammation and liver cell damage.

Alcoholic Cirrhosis: Severe scarring of the liver, leading to liver dysfunction and potentially liver failure.

Risk Factors

Several factors increase the risk of developing fatty liver disease, including:

Obesity: Excess body weight, especially abdominal obesity, is a significant risk factor.

Type 2 Diabetes: High blood sugar levels contribute to fat buildup in the liver.

Metabolic Syndrome: A cluster of conditions including high blood pressure, high blood sugar, excess body fat around the waist, and abnormal cholesterol levels.

High Cholesterol and Triglycerides: Elevated levels of fats in the blood can contribute to liver fat accumulation.

Poor Diet: Diets high in refined carbohydrates, sugary foods, and saturated fats.

Physical Inactivity: Lack of exercise can contribute to weight gain and insulin resistance.

Symptoms

Fatty liver disease often has no symptoms in its early stages. As the disease progresses, symptoms may include:

Fatigue

Weakness

Weight loss

Abdominal pain or discomfort, particularly in the upper right side

Enlarged liver

Jaundice (yellowing of the skin and eyes) in severe cases

The Basics of the Fatty Liver Diet: A Comprehensive Guide

The Fatty Liver Diet is a specialized diet designed to promote liver health, particularly for individuals with non-alcoholic fatty liver disease (NAFLD). This diet emphasizes nutrient-rich foods that help reduce liver fat, improve liver function, and support overall health.

Core Components of the Fatty Liver Diet

Lean Proteins: Incorporate sources like chicken, turkey, fish, beans, and legumes. These provide essential amino acids without the saturated fats that can exacerbate liver issues.

Healthy Fats: Focus on monounsaturated and polyunsaturated fats found in olive oil, avocados, nuts, and seeds. It's crucial to avoid trans fats and limit saturated fats, as these can harm your liver. By being mindful of these fats, you're taking a step towards better liver health. Complex Carbohydrates: Opt for whole grains such as brown rice, quinoa, oats, and whole wheat. These provide fiber and help regulate blood sugar levels.

Fruits and Vegetables: Aim for various colorful produce to ensure a wide range of vitamins, minerals, and antioxidants. Cruciferous vegetables like broccoli and Brussels sprouts are particularly beneficial.

Low Sugar Intake: Minimize the consumption of added sugars in sweets, sugary drinks, and processed foods.

Hydration: Remember, staying hydrated is key to maintaining a healthy liver. Drink plenty of water and limit alcohol consumption, as alcohol can further damage the liver. By committing to this, you're showing your dedication to your liver's well-being.

Health Benefits of the Fatty Liver Diet

The Fatty Liver Diet offers numerous health benefits, including:

Liver Health: This diet can improve liver function and potentially reverse NAFLD by reducing fat accumulation and inflammation in the liver.

Weight Management: The diet's emphasis on whole, nutrient-dense foods supports healthy weight loss and maintenance, which is crucial for liver health.

Reduced Risk of Chronic Diseases: A diet rich in fruits, vegetables, and healthy fats can lower the risk of heart disease, diabetes, and other chronic conditions.

Improved Digestion: The Fatty Liver Diet, emphasizing high-fiber foods, provides a reassuring boost to digestion and gut health, making it a reliable choice for those seeking digestive comfort.

Longevity: Consuming a balanced diet that supports liver health contributes to overall longevity and quality of life

Cultural Background

While the Fatty Liver Diet is rooted in modern nutritional science, it borrows elements from traditional Mediterranean and Asian diets, which are known for their emphasis on whole foods, healthy fats, and fresh produce. These cultures have long-valued meals that are both nutritious and enjoyed in a social context, promoting physical and emotional health.

Incorporating the Fatty Liver Diet into Daily Life

Transitioning to the Fatty Liver Diet can be simple with a few practical tips:

Meal Planning: Plan meals to ensure a balanced intake of lean proteins, healthy fats, and complex carbs. Batch cooking and meal prepping can save time and reduce the temptation to choose unhealthy options.

Shopping for Ingredients: Focus on the grocery store's perimeter, where fresh produce, meats, and dairy are typically found. Read labels to avoid added sugars and unhealthy fats.

Cooking Techniques: Use methods like grilling, baking, steaming, and sautéing with olive oil to preserve nutrients and avoid excess fat. Experiment with herbs and spices to enhance flavor without relying on salt or sugar.

Simple Swaps: Replace white rice with quinoa or cauliflower rice, choose whole grain bread over white bread, and snack on nuts or fruit instead of chips or sweets.

Embracing the Fatty Liver Lifestyle

Beyond the diet, the Fatty Liver lifestyle encourages regular physical activity and the social aspect of sharing meals. Walking, yoga, or strength training can enhance liver health and well-being. Additionally, sharing meals with family and friends can improve emotional health and create a positive relationship with food.

By adopting the Fatty Liver Diet and its associated lifestyle habits, you can take proactive steps towards better liver health, weight management, and a longer, more enjoyable life. Embrace the principles of this diet to experience the benefits of healthier and more balanced eating.

BREAKFAST

Healthy Shakshuka

 SERVES 4   **PREP TIME** 15 MIN.   **COOK TIME** 20 MIN.

Ingredients:
1 tablespoon olive oil
1 medium onion
1 red bell pepper
1 yellow bell pepper
2 cloves garlic, minced
1 teaspoon ground cumin
1 teaspoon paprika
1/2 teaspoon ground turmeric
1/4 teaspoon red pepper flakes
1 can (14.5 oz) diced tomatoes
1/2 cup tomato sauce, no salt added
1/4 cup water
4 large eggs
1/4 cup fresh parsley
Salt and pepper to taste

Nutritional Information (Per Serving):

Calories: 150

Protein: 8g

Carbohydrates: 14g

Fats: 7g

Fiber: 4g

Cholesterol: 186mg

Sodium: 300mg

Potassium: 400mg

Directions:
Wash and chop the onion, bell peppers, and garlic. Ensure all vegetables are finely chopped to help them cook evenly and quickly.

Heat the olive oil over medium heat in a large skillet. Add the chopped onion and bell peppers, and cook for about 5 minutes until they are softened. Stir in the minced garlic and cook for an additional 1 minute.

Add the ground cumin, paprika, ground turmeric, and red pepper flakes (if using) to the skillet. Stir well to coat the vegetables with the spices, cooking for about 1 minute to release their flavors.

Pour the diced tomatoes, tomato sauce, and water. Stir to combine. Bring the mixture to a simmer and cook for about 10 minutes, allowing the sauce to thicken slightly.

Use a spoon to make four small wells in the tomato mixture. Crack an egg into each well, ensuring the yolk remains intact. Reduce the heat to low, cover the skillet, and cook for about 7-10 minutes, or until the egg whites are set and the yolks are cooked to your liking. For runny yolks, cook for a shorter time; for firmer yolks, cook longer.

Serving Suggestions:
Pair with whole-grain bread or pita for added fiber.
Serve with a fresh green salad and a lemon vinaigrette.

Persian-Style Spinach & Herb Sauté with Eggs

 SERVES 4   **PREP TIME** 10 MIN.   **COOK TIME** 15 MIN.

Ingredients:
1 tablespoon olive oil
1 medium onion
2 cloves garlic
1 bunch fresh spinach
1/2 cup fresh parsley
1/2 cup fresh cilantro
1/2 cup fresh dill
1 teaspoon ground cumin
1/2 teaspoon ground turmeric
1/4 teaspoon ground black pepper
4 large eggs
Salt to taste
1/4 cup fresh lemon juice

Nutritional Information (Per Serving):

Calories: 160

Protein: 9g

Carbohydrates: 8g

Fats: 10g

Fiber: 3g

Cholesterol: 186mg

Sodium: 200mg

Potassium: 600mg

Directions:
Wash and chop the spinach, parsley, cilantro, and dill. Finely chop the onion and mince the garlic to ensure even cooking. Heat the olive oil over medium heat in a large non-stick skillet. Add the chopped onion and sauté for about 5 minutes, until translucent. Add the minced garlic and sauté for another minute until fragrant.

Add the chopped spinach, parsley, cilantro, and dill to the skillet. Stir well to combine. Add the ground cumin, ground turmeric, and ground black pepper. Sauté for about 5 minutes, until the spinach is wilted and the herbs are fragrant.

Use a spoon to make four small wells in the spinach mixture. Crack an egg into each well, ensuring the yolk remains intact. Cover the skillet and reduce the heat to low. Cook for about 5-7 minutes until the egg whites are set and the yolks are cooked to your liking.

Season with salt to taste. Drizzle fresh lemon juice over the dish. If using, sprinkle crumbled feta cheese on top.

Serving Suggestions:
Serve with whole-grain bread or a small side of brown rice for added fiber.
Pair with a fresh cucumber and tomato salad with lemon and olive oil.

BREAKFAST

Nutritious Zucchini Fritters

 SERVES 4   **PREP TIME** 15 MIN.   **COOK TIME** 20 MIN.

Ingredients:
3 medium zucchinis
1 teaspoon salt (for draining)
1 small onion
2 cloves garlic
1/2 cup whole wheat flour
1/4 cup rolled oats, finely ground
2 large eggs
1/4 cup fresh parsley
1/4 cup fresh dill
1 teaspoon ground cumin
1/2 teaspoon ground black pepper
1/4 teaspoon baking powder
1 tablespoon olive oil (for cooking)

Nutritional Information (Per Serving):

Calories: 150

Protein: 6g

Carbohydrates: 18g

Fats: 6g

Fiber: 4g

Cholesterol: 93mg

Sodium: 200mg

Potassium: 450mg

Directions:
Grate the zucchini and place them in a colander. Sprinkle with one teaspoon of salt and sit for 10 minutes to absorb excess moisture. After 10 minutes, squeeze the grated zucchini with your hands or use a clean kitchen towel to remove as much liquid as possible.

In a large mixing bowl, combine the grated zucchini, finely chopped onion, minced garlic, whole wheat flour, ground oats, lightly beaten eggs, chopped parsley, chopped dill, ground cumin, ground black pepper, and baking powder. Mix well until all ingredients are evenly distributed. If using, gently fold in the crumbled feta cheese.

Heat a non-stick skillet over medium heat and add one tablespoon of olive oil.

Scoop about two tablespoons of the zucchini mixture using a spoon or your hands and shape it into small patties. Gently place them in the heated skillet.

Cook the fritters for about 3-4 minutes on each side or until golden brown and cooked through. Avoid overcrowding the skillet; cook in batches if necessary. Add a little more olive oil if needed between batches.

Serving Suggestions:
Serve with a side of Greek yogurt or a light tzatziki sauce for dipping.
Pair with a fresh salad of mixed greens, tomatoes, and cucumbers.

Veggie Omelet with Spinach and Tomato

 SERVES 2   **PREP TIME** 10 MIN.   **COOK TIME** 10 MIN.

Ingredients:
4 large eggs
2 tablespoons water
1/4 teaspoon salt
1/4 teaspoon ground black pepper
1 tablespoon olive oil
1 small onion
1 cup fresh spinach
1 medium tomato
1/4 cup fresh parsley
1/4 cup fresh basil

Nutritional Information (Per Serving):

Calories: 220

Protein: 14g

Carbohydrates: 6g

Fats: 16g

Fiber: 2g

Cholesterol: 372mg

Sodium: 350mg

Potassium: 550mg

Directions:
Wash and chop the spinach, parsley, and basil. Dice the tomato and finely chop the onion.

In a medium bowl, whisk the eggs, water, salt, and ground black pepper until well combined and slightly frothy. The water helps make the omelet fluffier.

Heat the olive oil over medium heat in a non-stick skillet. Add the chopped onion and sauté for about 3 minutes until it becomes translucent. Add the chopped spinach and diced tomato to the skillet and cook for another 2-3 minutes until the spinach is wilted and the tomatoes are slightly softened.

Pour the egg mixture over the vegetables in the skillet. Gently stir the mixture to distribute the vegetables evenly throughout the eggs. Allow the eggs to cook undisturbed for about 2-3 minutes or until the edges start to set.

Sprinkle the chopped parsley, basil, and optional feta cheese over one-half of the omelet. Using a spatula, carefully fold the other half of the omelet over the herbs and cheese. Cook for another 1-2 minutes until the omelet is fully set but still moist.

Serving Suggestions:
Serve with a side of fresh fruit or a small green salad.
Pair with whole-grain toast for added fiber

BREAKFAST

Scrambled Tofu with Mushrooms and Peppers

 SERVES 4 **PREP TIME** 10 MIN. **COOK TIME** 15 MIN.

Ingredients:
1 tablespoon olive oil
1 medium onion
2 cloves garlic
1 red bell pepper
1 yellow bell pepper
1 cup mushrooms
1 block (14 oz) firm tofu
1 teaspoon ground turmeric
1 teaspoon ground cumin
1/2 teaspoon ground black pepper
1/4 teaspoon salt
1/4 cup fresh parsley
1/4 cup fresh cilantro

Nutritional Information (Per Serving):
Calories: 170
Protein: 14g
Carbohydrates: 12g
Fats: 9g
Fiber: 4g
Cholesterol: 0mg
Sodium: 250mg
Potassium: 500mg

Directions:
Wash and chop the onion, bell peppers, mushrooms, parsley, and cilantro. Drain and crumble the tofu with your hands or using a fork.

Heat the olive oil over medium heat in a large, non-stick skillet. Add the chopped onion and sauté for about 3-4 minutes until it becomes translucent. Add the minced garlic and cook for another 1 minute.

Add the chopped red and yellow bell peppers and the sliced mushrooms to the skillet. Sauté for about 5 minutes until the vegetables are tender.

Add the crumbled tofu to the skillet. Stir well to combine with the vegetables. Add the ground turmeric, ground cumin, ground black pepper, and salt. Cook for 5-7 minutes, stirring occasionally, until the tofu is heated and slightly browned.

Sprinkle the nutritional yeast over the tofu mixture and stir well. Add the chopped parsley and cilantro, stirring to combine. Cook for 1-2 minutes until the herbs are wilted and fragrant.

Serving Suggestions:
Serve with whole-grain toast or a small serving of brown rice. Pair with a fresh salad of mixed greens and a light vinaigrette.

Avocado Toast with Poached Egg

 SERVES 2 **PREP TIME** 10 MIN. **COOK TIME** 10 MIN.

Ingredients:
2 slices whole grain bread
1 ripe avocado
2 large eggs
1 tablespoon lemon juice
1/4 teaspoon ground black pepper
1/4 teaspoon salt
Fresh herbs for garnish
(e.g., parsley, cilantro)

Nutritional Information (Per Serving):
Calories: 220
Protein: 14g
Carbohydrates: 6g
Fats: 16g
Fiber: 2g
Cholesterol: 372mg
Sodium: 350mg
Potassium: 550mg

Directions:
Toast the whole grain bread slices to your desired level of crispness.

While the bread is toasting, cut the avocado in half, remove the pit, and scoop the flesh into a bowl. Add the lemon juice, ground black pepper, and salt. Mash the avocado with a fork until it reaches a creamy consistency.

Poach Eggs:
Fill a medium saucepan with about 3 inches of water and simmer over medium heat.

Crack each egg into a small bowl or ramekin.

Using a spoon, create a gentle whirlpool in the water and carefully slide one egg into the center of the whirlpool. This helps the egg whites wrap around the yolk. Repeat with the second egg.

Let the eggs poach for about 3-4 minutes until the whites are set, but the yolks are still runny. Use a slotted spoon to carefully remove the eggs from the water and place them on a paper towel to drain excess water.

Spread the mashed avocado evenly over the toasted bread slices.

Place a poached egg on top of each slice of avocado toast.

Optionally, drizzle a small amount of olive oil on top for added flavor and healthy fats.

Serving Suggestions:
Serve with a side of fresh fruit or a simple green salad.
Add sliced tomatoes or radishes on top for extra flavor and nutrients.

BREAKFAST

Hummus and Veggie Breakfast Wrap

 SERVES 2   **PREP TIME** 10 MIN.   **COOK TIME** 5 MIN.

Ingredients:
2 whole grain tortillas
1/2 cup hummus
1/2 cup baby spinach leaves
1/4 cup shredded carrots
1/2 cup cucumber
1/2 red bell pepper
1/4 cup cherry tomatoes
1/4 cup red onion
1 tablespoon lemon juice
1/4 teaspoon ground black pepper
1/4 teaspoon salt

Nutritional Information (Per Serving):
Calories: 220
Protein: 8g
Carbohydrates: 32g
Fats: 8g
Fiber: 8g
Cholesterol: 0mg
Sodium: 350mg
Potassium: 550mg

Directions:
Wash and prepare the baby spinach, shredded carrots, cucumber, red bell pepper, cherry tomatoes, and red onion. Ensure all vegetables are thinly sliced for easy wrapping and even distribution.

In a medium bowl, combine the sliced cucumber, red bell pepper, cherry tomatoes, and red onion. Drizzle with lemon juice, and sprinkle with ground black pepper and salt. Toss to combine and set aside.

Warm the whole grain tortillas in a non-stick skillet over medium heat for about 1 minute on each side or until they are pliable and warm. Alternatively, you can warm them in a microwave for about 15-20 seconds.

Lay each warmed tortilla flat on a clean surface. Spread 1/4 cup of hummus evenly over each tortilla, leaving about an inch of space around the edges.

Layer half of the baby spinach leaves, shredded carrots, seasoned vegetable mixture, and optional fresh parsley or cilantro over the hummus on each tortilla.

Fold in the sides of the tortilla and then roll it up tightly from the bottom to the top, creating a wrap. Slice each wrap in half if desired.

Serving Suggestions:
Serve with whole-grain toast or a small serving of brown rice. Pair with a fresh salad of mixed greens and a light vinaigrette.

Millet Porridge with Almond Milk and Pears

 SERVES 4   **PREP TIME** 10 MIN. **COOK TIME** 25 MIN.

Ingredients:
1 cup millet
3 cups unsweetened almond milk
1 cup water
2 medium pears, diced
1 tablespoon maple syrup (optional)
1 teaspoon ground cinnamon
1/2 teaspoon ground ginger
1/4 teaspoon ground nutmeg
1/4 teaspoon salt
1 teaspoon vanilla extract

Nutritional Information (Per Serving):
Calories: 210
Protein: 5g
Carbohydrates: 40g
Fats: 4g
Fiber: 6g
Cholesterol: 0mg
Sodium: 150mg
Potassium: 250mg

Directions:
Place the millet in a fine mesh strainer and rinse under cold water until the water runs clear. This helps remove any residual bitterness.

In a medium saucepan, combine the rinsed millet, almond milk, and water. Bring to a boil over medium-high heat, then reduce the heat to low and simmer, covered, for about 20 minutes, or until the millet is tender and the liquid is absorbed. Stir occasionally to prevent sticking.

While the millet is cooking, wash and dice the pears. You can leave the skin on for added fiber and nutrients.

Once the millet is cooked, stir in the diced pears, maple syrup (if using), ground cinnamon, ground ginger, ground nutmeg, salt, and vanilla extract. Cook for an additional 5 minutes, stirring frequently, until the pears are slightly softened and the porridge is creamy.

Serving Suggestions:
Serve warm with an additional splash of almond milk if a creamier consistency is desired.

Top with a handful of fresh berries or a drizzle of honey for added flavor.

BREAKFAST

Oatmeal with Almonds and Blueberries

 SERVES 2   **PREP TIME** 5 MIN.   **COOK TIME** 10 MIN.

Ingredients:
1 cup old-fashioned rolled oats
2 cups unsweetened almond milk
1 tablespoon chia seeds
1 tablespoon flax seeds, ground
1/2 teaspoon ground cinnamon
1/4 teaspoon ground nutmeg
1/4 teaspoon salt
1 teaspoon vanilla extract

1 cup fresh blueberries

Nutritional Information (Per Serving):
Calories: 270
Protein: 8g
Carbohydrates: 45g
Fats: 9g
Fiber: 10g
Cholesterol: 0mg
Sodium: 150mg
Potassium: 300mg

Directions:
In a medium saucepan, combine the rolled oats, almond milk, chia seeds, ground flaxseeds, ground cinnamon, ground nutmeg, and salt. Bring to a boil over medium-high heat, then reduce the heat to low and simmer, stirring occasionally, for about 5-7 minutes, or until the oats are tender and the mixture is creamy.
Stir in the vanilla extract and cook for another minute.
While the oatmeal is cooking, wash the blueberries and chop the almonds.

Serving Suggestions:
Serve with fresh fruit or a small green smoothie for added nutrients.
Add a dollop of Greek yogurt on top for extra protein.

Baked Apple and Cinnamon Oatmeal

 SERVES 4   **PREP TIME** 15 MIN.   **COOK TIME** 35 MIN.

Ingredients:
2 cups old-fashioned rolled oats
1 teaspoon ground cinnamon
1/2 teaspoon ground nutmeg
1/4 teaspoon ground ginger
1/4 teaspoon salt
1 teaspoon baking powder
2 cups unsweetened almond milk
1/2 cup unsweetened applesauce
1 teaspoon vanilla extract
2 medium apples, peeled, cored, and diced

Nutritional Information (Per Serving):
Calories: 220
Protein: 5g
Carbohydrates: 39g
Fats: 5g
Fiber: 6g
Cholesterol: 0mg
Sodium: 200mg
Potassium: 300mg

Directions:
Preheat your oven to 350°F (175°C). Lightly grease an 8x8-inch baking dish with a small amount of olive oil or cooking spray.
In a large mixing bowl, combine the rolled oats, ground cinnamon, ground nutmeg, ground ginger, salt, and baking powder. Mix well to distribute the spices and baking powder evenly.
In another bowl, whisk together the unsweetened almond milk, unsweetened applesauce, maple syrup (if using), and vanilla extract.
Pour the wet ingredients into the bowl with the dry ingredients and stir until thoroughly combined. Fold in the diced apples.
Pour the oatmeal mixture into the prepared baking dish. Spread it out evenly and sprinkle the chopped walnuts on top if using. Bake in the preheated oven for 30-35 minutes or until the oatmeal is set and the top is golden brown.

Serving Suggestions:
Serve warm with a splash of almond milk or a dollop of Greek yogurt.
Add a side of fresh fruit or a small green smoothie for added nutrients.

BREAKFAST

Sweet Potato and Black Bean Breakfast Burrito

 SERVES 4   **PREP TIME** 15 MIN.   **COOK TIME** 25 MIN.

Ingredients:
2 medium sweet potatoes
1 tablespoon olive oil
1 small onion
2 cloves garlic
1 red bell pepper
1 can (15 oz) black beans
1 teaspoon ground cumin
1/2 teaspoon smoked paprika
1/2 teaspoon ground black pepper
1/4 teaspoon salt
4 large whole-grain tortillas
1/2 cup fresh cilantro

Nutritional Information (Per Serving):

Calories: 300

Protein: 10g

Carbohydrates: 50g

Fats: 7g

Fiber: 12g

Cholesterol: 0mg

Sodium: 400mg

Potassium: 700mg

Directions:
In a medium saucepan, add the diced sweet potatoes and enough water to cover them. Bring to a boil and cook for about 10 minutes or until the sweet potatoes are tender. Drain and set aside.

Heat the olive oil over medium heat in a large, non-stick skillet. Add the chopped onion and sauté for about 3-4 minutes until it becomes translucent. Add the minced garlic and diced red bell pepper, and cook for another 3-4 minutes until the peppers are tender.

Add the drained black beans and cooked sweet potatoes to the skillet. Stir to combine.

Add the ground cumin, smoked paprika, black pepper, and salt. Stir well and cook for another 3-4 minutes until everything is heated and the flavors are well combined.

Warm the whole grain tortillas in a non-stick skillet over medium heat for about 1 minute on each side or until they are pliable and warm. Alternatively, you can warm them in a microwave for about 15-20 seconds.

Lay each warmed tortilla flat on a clean surface. Divide the sweet potato and black bean mixture evenly among the tortillas. Top with chopped cilantro, optional salsa, and avocado slices.

Fold in the sides of the tortilla and then roll it up tightly from the bottom to the top, creating a burrito. Slice each burrito in half if desired.

Serving Suggestions:
Serve with fresh fruit or a small green smoothie for added nutrients.
Add a dollop of Greek yogurt on the side for extra protein.

Chickpea Flour Crepes

 SERVES 4   **PREP TIME** 10 MIN.   **COOK TIME** 20 MIN.

Ingredients:
1 cup chickpea flour (also known as besan or garbanzo bean flour)
1 1/4 cups water
1/4 teaspoon salt
1/4 teaspoon ground turmeric
1/4 teaspoon ground cumin
1 tablespoon olive oil (for cooking)

Nutritional Information (Per Serving):

Calories: 130

Protein: 6g

Carbohydrates: 18g

Fats: 3g

Fiber: 3g

Cholesterol: 0mg

Sodium: 150mg

Potassium: 240mg

Directions:
In a medium bowl, whisk the chickpea flour, water, salt, turmeric, and ground cumin until smooth. The batter should be thin and soft, similar to pancake batter. Let the batter rest for 10 minutes to allow the flour to hydrate fully.

Heat a non-stick skillet or crepe pan over medium heat. Lightly grease the pan with a small amount of olive oil using a brush or paper towel.

Cook Crepes:

Pour about 1/4 cup of batter into the center of the pan. Quickly swirl the pan to spread the batter evenly into a thin layer.

Cook for 1-2 minutes until the edges lift and the bottom is golden brown. Flip the crepe and cook on the other side for 1-2 minutes.

Remove the crepe from the pan and place it on a plate.

Repeat with the remaining batter, lightly greasing the pan as needed.

Serving Suggestions:
Serve with a filling of fresh vegetables, such as spinach, tomatoes, and avocado, or a dollop of Greek yogurt.

BREAKFAST

Smoothie Bowl with Fresh Strawberries

 SERVES 2   **PREP TIME** 10 MIN.   **COOK TIME** NONE

Ingredients:

1 cup frozen strawberries
1 medium banana, sliced and frozen
1/2 cup unsweetened almond milk
1/2 cup plain Greek yogurt
1 tablespoon chia seeds
1 tablespoon flax seeds, ground
1 teaspoon vanilla extract
1 cup fresh strawberries
1/4 cup granola (low-sugar, for topping)
2 tablespoons chopped almonds

(for topping)

> **Nutritional Information (Per Serving):**
> Calories: 280
> Protein: 10g
> Carbohydrates: 40g
> Fats: 10g
> Fiber: 10g
> Cholesterol: 0mg
> Sodium: 100mg
> Potassium: 500mg

Directions:

In a blender, combine the frozen strawberries, frozen banana, unsweetened almond milk, plain Greek yogurt, chia seeds, ground flaxseeds, and vanilla extract. Blend until smooth and creamy. If the mixture is too thick, add more almond milk to reach your desired consistency.
Divide the smoothie mixture evenly between two bowls.
Top each bowl with fresh sliced strawberries, granola, and chopped almonds. Garnish with fresh mint leaves if desired.

Serving Suggestions:

Enjoy the smoothie bowl as a nutritious breakfast or a refreshing snack.
Pair with a whole-grain toast or a boiled egg for added protein.

Buckwheat Pancakes with Maple Syrup and Berry Seeds

 SERVES 4   **PREP TIME** 8 MIN.   **COOK TIME** 20 MIN.

Ingredients:

1 cup buckwheat flour
1 tablespoon ground flaxseeds
2 tablespoons chia seeds
1 teaspoon baking powder
1/4 teaspoon salt
1 cup unsweetened almond milk
1 tablespoon maple syrup (plus extra for serving)
1 teaspoon vanilla extract
1 large egg
1 tablespoon olive oil (for cooking)
1 cup mixed berries (e.g., strawberries, blueberries, raspberries)
2 tablespoons sunflower seeds (optional for topping)

> **Nutritional Information (Per Serving):**
> Calories: 250
> Protein: 7g
> Carbohydrates: 38g
> Fats: 8g
> Fiber: 7g
> Cholesterol: 50mg
> Sodium: 150mg
> Potassium: 200mg

Directions:

In a large mixing bowl, combine the buckwheat flour, ground flaxseeds, chia seeds, baking powder, and salt. Mix well.
In another bowl, whisk together the unsweetened almond milk, one tablespoon of maple syrup, vanilla extract, and the egg until well combined.
Pour the wet ingredients into the bowl with the dry ingredients. Stir until just combined. Let the batter rest for 5 minutes to let the chia seeds thicken the mixture slightly.
Heat a non-stick skillet or griddle over medium heat and lightly grease with olive oil.
Cook Pancakes:
Pour about 1/4 cup of batter onto the skillet for each pancake. Cook for 2-3 minutes until bubbles form on the surface and the edges look set.
Flip the pancakes and cook for another 1-2 minutes until golden brown and cooked through. Adjust the heat as needed to prevent burning.

Serving Suggestions:

Serve with a side of Greek yogurt for added protein.
Enjoy with a green smoothie or fresh fruit salad for a balanced breakfast.

BREAKFAST

Cottage Cheese with Pineapple and Flax

 SERVES 2   **PREP TIME** 5 MIN.   **COOK TIME** NONE

Ingredients:
1 cup low-fat cottage cheese
1 cup fresh pineapple, diced
1 tablespoon ground flaxseeds

Nutritional Information (Per Serving):

Calories: 160

Protein: 12g

Carbohydrates: 20g

Fats: 3g

Fiber: 3g

Cholesterol: 10mg

Sodium: 400mg

Potassium: 350mg

Directions:
Dice the fresh pineapple into small, bite-sized pieces.
In a medium bowl, combine the low-fat cottage cheese, diced pineapple, and ground flaxseeds. Stir well to mix.
Drizzle the honey over the mixture and sprinkle with ground cinnamon. Stir gently to combine.

Serving Suggestions:
Serve as a nutritious breakfast or a healthy snack.
Pair with a whole-grain toast or a handful of mixed nuts for added nutrients.

Greek Yogurt with Honey and Walnuts

 SERVES 2   **PREP TIME** 5 MIN. **COOK TIME** NONE

Ingredients:
1 cup low-fat Greek yogurt
2 tablespoons honey
1/4 cup walnuts

Nutritional Information (Per Serving):

Calories: 220

Protein: 14g

Carbohydrates: 24g

Fats: 10g

Fiber: 2g

Cholesterol: 5mg

Sodium: 60mg

Potassium: 250mg

Directions:
Chop the walnuts into small pieces.
In a medium bowl, mix the low-fat Greek yogurt with the vanilla extract (if using) until smooth and well combined.
Divide the Greek yogurt into two serving bowls.
Drizzle one tablespoon of honey over each bowl of yogurt.
Sprinkle each with two tablespoons of chopped walnuts and a pinch of ground cinnamon (if using).

Serving Suggestions:
Serve as a nutritious breakfast or a healthy snack.
Pair with a side of fresh fruit or a small whole-grain muffin for added nutrients.

BREAKFAST

Banana and Oat Pancakes

 SERVES 4 **PREP TIME** 10 MIN. **COOK TIME** 15 MIN.

Ingredients:

2 medium ripe bananas
2 large eggs
1 cup rolled oats
1/2 cup unsweetened almond milk
1 teaspoon vanilla extract
1 teaspoon ground cinnamon
1 teaspoon baking powder
1/4 teaspoon salt
1 tablespoon olive oil (for cooking)

Nutritional Information (Per Serving):

Calories: 220
Protein: 6g
Carbohydrates: 34g
Fats: 7g
Fiber: 4g
Cholesterol: 55mg
Sodium: 250mg
Potassium: 450mg

Directions:

In a blender, combine the bananas, eggs, rolled oats, almond milk, vanilla extract, ground cinnamon, baking powder, and salt. Blend until the mixture is smooth and well combined. Let the batter rest for 5 minutes to thicken slightly.

Heat a non-stick skillet or griddle over medium heat. Lightly grease the pan with a small amount of olive oil.

Cook Pancakes:

Pour about 1/4 cup of batter onto the skillet for each pancake. Cook for 2-3 minutes until bubbles form on the surface and the edges look set.

Flip the pancakes and cook for another 1-2 minutes until golden brown and cooked through. Adjust the heat as needed to prevent burning.

Serving Suggestions:

Serve with a side of Greek yogurt or a dollop of almond butter for added protein.

Enjoy with a green smoothie or fresh fruit salad for a balanced breakfast.

Blueberry Almond Pancakes

 SERVES 4 **PREP TIME** 10 MIN. **COOK TIME** 15 MIN.

Ingredients:

1 cup rolled oats
1/2 cup almond flour
1 teaspoon baking powder
1/2 teaspoon baking soda
1/4 teaspoon salt
1 teaspoon ground cinnamon
2 large eggs
1 cup unsweetened almond milk
1 teaspoon vanilla extract
1 cup fresh or frozen blueberries
1/4 cup sliced almonds
1 tablespoon olive oil (for cooking)

Nutritional Information (Per Serving):

Calories: 250
Protein: 8g
Carbohydrates: 30g
Fats: 10g
Fiber: 5g
Cholesterol: 55mg
Sodium: 220mg
Potassium: 350mg

Directions:

In a large mixing bowl, combine the rolled oats, almond flour, baking powder, baking soda, salt, and ground cinnamon. Mix well to ensure even distribution.

In another bowl, whisk together the eggs, almond milk, honey, or maple syrup (if using), and vanilla extract until well combined.

Pour the wet ingredients into the dry ingredients and stir until combined. Fold in the blueberries and sliced almonds gently to avoid breaking the berries. Let the batter rest for 5 minutes to thicken slightly.

Heat a non-stick skillet or griddle over medium heat and lightly grease with olive oil.

Cook Pancakes:

Pour about 1/4 cup of batter onto the skillet for each pancake. Cook for 2-3 minutes until bubbles form on the surface and the edges look set.

Flip the pancakes and cook for another 1-2 minutes until golden brown and cooked through. Adjust the heat as needed to prevent burning.

Serving Suggestions:

Serve with a side of Greek yogurt or a dollop of almond butter for added protein.

Enjoy with a green smoothie or fresh fruit salad for a balanced breakfast.

BREAKFAST

Quinoa and Berry Bowl

 SERVES 2   **PREP TIME** 10 MIN.   **COOK TIME** 15 MIN.

Ingredients:
1/2 cup quinoa
1 cup water
1 cup unsweetened almond milk
1 tablespoon chia seeds
1 tablespoon ground flaxseeds
1 teaspoon vanilla extract
1 cup mixed berries (e.g., blueberries, strawberries, raspberries)
2 tablespoons sliced almonds

Nutritional Information (Per Serving):

Calories: 280

Protein: 8g

Carbohydrates: 40g

Fats: 10g

Fiber: 10g

Cholesterol: 0mg

Sodium: 60mg

Potassium: 450mg

Directions:
Rinse the quinoa under cold water using a fine mesh strainer. In a medium saucepan, combine the quinoa and water. Bring to a boil over medium-high heat, then reduce the heat to low, cover, and simmer for 12-15 minutes until the quinoa is tender and the water is absorbed. Remove from heat and let it sit, covered, for 5 minutes, then fluff with a fork.
While the quinoa is cooking, in a small bowl, mix the unsweetened almond milk, chia seeds, ground flaxseeds, and vanilla extract. Stir well and let it sit for about 5 minutes to allow the chia seeds to thicken.
Add it to a large mixing bowl once the quinoa is cooked and fluffed. Pour the almond milk mixture over the quinoa and stir until well combined.
Gently fold in the mixed berries. Drizzle the maple syrup over the mixture and stir gently to combine.

Serving Suggestions:
Serve as a nutritious breakfast or a healthy snack.
Pair with a side of Greek yogurt or a small green smoothie for added nutrients

Chia Seed Pudding with Fresh Fruit

 SERVES 4   **PREP TIME** 10 MIN.   **COOK TIME** 4 HOURS

Ingredients:
1/2 cup chia seeds
2 cups unsweetened almond milk
1 teaspoon vanilla extract
1 cup fresh fruit, chopped (e.g., strawberries, blueberries, mango, kiwi)

Nutritional Information (Per Serving):

Calories: 180

Protein: 5g

Carbohydrates: 18g

Fats: 10g

Fiber: 12g

Cholesterol: 0mg

Sodium: 60mg

Potassium: 300mg

Directions:
In a medium bowl, whisk together the chia seeds, unsweetened almond milk, maple syrup (if using), and vanilla extract until well combined.
Cover the bowl and refrigerate for at least 4 hours or overnight. Stir the mixture once or twice during the first hour to prevent clumping.
While the pudding is chilling, wash and chop the fresh fruit into bite-sized pieces.
Stir it well once the chia pudding has set and thickened. Divide the pudding into four serving bowls. If desired, top each bowl with the chopped fresh fruit and a sprinkle of sliced almonds.
Garnish with fresh mint leaves if desired.

Serving Suggestions:
Pair with a small side of Greek yogurt for added protein

BREAKFAST

Egg White and Veggie Frittata

 SERVES 4   **PREP TIME** 10 MIN.   **COOK TIME** 20 MIN.

Ingredients:

2 cups egg whites
(about 12 large egg whites)
1/2 cup unsweetened almond milk
1 tablespoon olive oil
1 small onion
1 red bell pepper
1 zucchini
1 cup baby spinach
1/2 cup cherry tomatoes
1/4 cup fresh parsley
1/4 teaspoon salt
1/4 teaspoon ground black pepper
1/4 teaspoon garlic powder
1/4 teaspoon paprika

Nutritional Information (Per Serving):

Calories: 110
Protein: 15g
Carbohydrates: 6g
Fats: 3g
Fiber: 2g
Cholesterol: 0mg
Sodium: 250mg
Potassium: 400mg

Directions:

Preheat your oven to 375°F (190°C). Lightly grease a 9-inch ovenproof skillet or baking dish with olive oil.
Heat the olive oil over medium heat in a large, non-stick skillet. Add the chopped onion, red bell pepper, and sauté for 3-4 minutes until softened. Add the zucchini and continue to cook for another 3 minutes. Stir in the chopped spinach and cook until wilted about 2 minutes. Remove from heat.
In a large bowl, whisk together the egg whites, unsweetened almond milk, salt, ground black pepper, garlic powder, and paprika.
Add the sautéed vegetables to the egg mixture and stir to combine. Pour the mixture into the prepared skillet or baking dish. Scatter the halved cherry tomatoes on top.
Place the skillet or baking dish in the oven and bake for 20-25 minutes until the frittata is set and lightly golden on top. A toothpick inserted into the center should come out clean.

Serving Suggestions:

Serve with a side of mixed greens or a fresh fruit salad.
Pair with whole-grain toast or a small serving of quinoa for added fiber and nutrients.

Omelet with Zucchini and Herbs

 SERVES 2   **PREP TIME** 10 MIN.   **COOK TIME** 10 MIN.

Ingredients:

4 large egg whites
2 large eggs
1/4 cup unsweetened almond milk
1 medium zucchini
1 small onion
1 tablespoon olive oil
1/4 cup fresh parsley
1/4 cup fresh basil
1/4 teaspoon salt
1/4 teaspoon ground black pepper
1/4 teaspoon garlic powder

Nutritional Information (Per Serving):

Calories: 150
Protein: 15g
Carbohydrates: 6g
Fats: 7g
Fiber: 2g
Cholesterol: 110mg
Sodium: 200mg
Potassium: 400mg

Directions:

Grate the zucchini and finely chop the onion and fresh herbs.
In a medium bowl, whisk the egg whites, eggs, and unsweetened almond milk until well combined. Add the salt, ground black pepper, and garlic powder to the egg mixture and whisk again.
Heat the olive oil over medium heat in a non-stick skillet. Add the chopped onion and sauté for about 3 minutes until softened. Add the grated zucchini and cook for another 2-3 minutes until the zucchini is tender and any excess moisture has evaporated.
Cook Omelet:
Pour the egg mixture into the skillet over the sautéed vegetables. Tilt the skillet to ensure the eggs cover the vegetables evenly.
Cook the omelet on medium-low heat until the edges start to set and the center is still slightly runny for about 3-4 minutes. Sprinkle the chopped parsley and basil over one-half of the omelet.
Gently fold the omelet in half using a spatula. Continue cooking for another 1-2 minutes until the omelet is cooked through but still moist inside.

Serving Suggestions:

Serve with mixed greens or a small fruit salad for added fiber and nutrients.
Pair with whole-grain toast or a small serving of quinoa for a complete meal.

BREAKFAST

Vegan Waffles

 SERVES 4　 **PREP TIME** 10 MIN.　 **COOK TIME** 20 MIN.

Ingredients:
1 1/2 cups whole wheat flour
1/2 cup rolled oats, finely ground
2 tablespoons ground flaxseeds
1 tablespoon baking powder
1/2 teaspoon salt
1 teaspoon ground cinnamon
1 1/2 cups unsweetened almond milk
1/4 cup unsweetened applesauce
1 teaspoon vanilla extract
1 tablespoon olive oil
(for greasing the waffle iron)

Nutritional Information (Per Serving):

Calories: 200

Protein: 6g

Carbohydrates: 36g

Fats: 4g

Fiber: 6g

Cholesterol: 0mg

Sodium: 300mg

Potassium: 200mg

Directions:
In a large mixing bowl, combine the whole wheat flour, ground oats, ground flaxseeds, baking powder, salt, and ground cinnamon. Mix well to ensure even distribution of ingredients.
In another bowl, whisk together the unsweetened almond milk, unsweetened applesauce, maple syrup (if using), and vanilla extract until well combined.
Pour the wet ingredients into the bowl with the dry ingredients. Stir until just combined. Let the batter rest for 5 minutes to let the flaxseeds thicken the mixture slightly.
Preheat your waffle iron according to the manufacturer's instructions. Lightly grease the waffle iron with a small amount of olive oil using a brush or paper towel.
Cook Waffles:
Pour about 1/4 cup of batter onto the preheated waffle iron for each waffle.
Close the waffle iron and cook according to the manufacturer's instructions, typically 3-5 minutes, until the waffles are golden brown and crisp.
Repeat with the remaining batter, lightly greasing the waffle iron as needed.

Serving Suggestions:
Top with fresh berries, sliced bananas, or a drizzle of maple syrup.
Serve with a side of fresh fruit or a green smoothie for added nutrients.

Banana & Tahini Porridge

 SERVES 2　 **PREP TIME** 5 MIN.　 **COOK TIME** 10 MIN.

Ingredients:
1 cup rolled oats
2 cups unsweetened almond milk
1 medium banana, sliced
1 tablespoon tahini
1 tablespoon chia seeds
1/2 teaspoon ground cinnamon
1/4 teaspoon ground nutmeg
1/4 teaspoon vanilla extract

Nutritional Information (Per Serving):

Calories: 250

Protein: 7g

Carbohydrates: 38g

Fats: 9g

Fiber: 7g

Cholesterol: 0mg

Sodium: 70mg

Potassium: 450mg

Directions:
In a medium saucepan, combine the rolled oats, unsweetened almond milk, sliced banana, tahini, chia seeds, ground cinnamon, and ground nutmeg.
Place the saucepan over medium heat. Bring the mixture to a gentle boil, then reduce the heat to low and simmer for about 10 minutes, stirring frequently, until the oats are tender and the porridge is creamy. If the porridge becomes too thick, add more almond milk to reach your desired consistency.
Stir in the vanilla extract and optional maple syrup. Mix well.

Serving Suggestions:
Top with fresh berries, sliced kiwi, or a handful of chopped nuts for added texture and flavor.
Serve with a side of Greek yogurt for added protein.

BREAKFAST

Nutritious Curried Broccoli & Boiled Eggs on Toast

 SERVES 2   **PREP TIME** 10 MIN.   **COOK TIME** 20 MIN.

Ingredients:
4 large eggs
2 cups broccoli florets
1 tablespoon olive oil
1 small onion
1 garlic clove
1 teaspoon curry powder
1/2 teaspoon ground turmeric
1/4 teaspoon ground cumin
1/4 teaspoon salt
1/4 teaspoon ground black pepper
4 slices whole grain bread

Nutritional Information (Per Serving):

Calories: 320

Protein: 20g

Carbohydrates: 32g

Fats: 12g

Fiber: 8g

Cholesterol: 370mg

Sodium: 400mg

Potassium: 550mg

Directions:
Place the eggs in a saucepan and cover them with cold water. Once cooled, peel the eggs and slice them.

While the eggs are boiling, steam the broccoli florets until tender, about 5 minutes. Alternatively, blanch them in boiling water for 2-3 minutes and then drain.

Heat the olive oil over medium heat in a large skillet. Add the finely chopped onion and sauté for 3-4 minutes until translucent. Add the minced garlic and cook for another minute until fragrant.

Add the curry powder, ground turmeric, ground cumin, salt, and ground black pepper to the skillet. Stir well to coat the onions and garlic with the spices. Add the steamed broccoli and toss to combine, cooking for another 2-3 minutes until the broccoli is well-coated and heated through.

Toast the slices of whole grain bread to your desired level of crispness.

Place the toasted bread on plates. Top each slice with the curried broccoli mixture, and then arrange the sliced boiled eggs on top.

Serving Suggestions:
Serve with a side of fresh fruit or a small green salad.
Add a dollop of Greek yogurt on the side for added protein.

SOUP AND STEW

Beet and Carrot Soup

 SERVES 4   **PREP TIME** 15 MIN.   **COOK TIME** 30 MIN.

Ingredients:
2 medium beets, peeled and diced
3 large carrots, peeled and sliced
1 medium onion
2 cloves garlic
1 tablespoon olive oil
4 cups low-sodium vegetable broth
1 teaspoon ground cumin
1/2 teaspoon ground coriander
1/4 teaspoon ground turmeric
1/4 teaspoon ground black pepper
1/2 teaspoon salt
1 tablespoon lemon juice

Nutritional Information (Per Serving):

Calories: 130

Protein: 3g

Carbohydrates: 24g

Fats: 3g

Fiber: 5g

Cholesterol: 0mg

Sodium: 350mg

Potassium: 550mg

Directions:
Peel and dice the beets, peel and slice the carrots, and chop the onion. Mince the garlic.

Heat the olive oil over medium heat in a large pot. Add the chopped onion and sauté for about 5 minutes until translucent. Add the minced garlic and cook for another minute until fragrant.

Add the diced and sliced carrots to the pot. Stir to combine with the onions and garlic.

Sprinkle the ground cumin, ground coriander, ground turmeric, ground black pepper, and salt over the vegetables.

Pour in the low-sodium vegetable broth. Bring the mixture to a boil, then reduce the heat to low, cover, and simmer for about 25 minutes or until the beets and carrots are tender.

Use an immersion blender to puree the soup until smooth. Alternatively, you can carefully transfer the soup in batches to a blender and blend until smooth. Return the blended soup to the pot.

Stir in the lemon juice for a fresh flavor.

Serving Suggestions:
Serve with a side of whole-grain bread or a small green salad.

Top with a dollop of Greek yogurt for added creaminess and protein.

Butternut Squash Soup

 SERVES 4   **PREP TIME** 15 MIN.   **COOK TIME** 30 MIN.

Ingredients:
1 medium butternut squash
(about 2 pounds), peeled, seeded, and cubed
1 tablespoon olive oil
1 large onion
2 cloves garlic
4 cups low-sodium vegetable broth
1 teaspoon ground ginger
1/2 teaspoon ground cinnamon
1/4 teaspoon ground nutmeg
Salt and black pepper to taste

Nutritional Information (Per Serving):

Calories: 180

Protein: 3g

Carbohydrates: 35g

Fats: 4g

Fiber: 6g

Cholesterol: 0mg

Sodium: 300mg

Potassium: 900mg

Directions:
Peel, seed, and cube the butternut squash. Set aside.

Heat the olive oil over medium heat in a large pot. Add the diced onion and sauté until translucent, about 5 minutes. Add the minced garlic and sauté for another minute until fragrant.

Add the cubed butternut squash to the pot and stir to mix with the onion and garlic. Cook for about 5 minutes, stirring occasionally.

Add the ground ginger, ground cinnamon, ground nutmeg, and cayenne pepper if using.

Pour in the low-sodium vegetable broth. Bring the mixture to a boil, then reduce the heat to low and simmer for about 20 minutes or until the squash is tender and can be easily pierced with a fork.

Once the squash is soft, use an immersion blender to purée the soup directly in the pot until smooth. Alternatively, carefully transfer the soup in batches to a blender and blend until soft, then return to the pot.

Taste the soup and add salt, black pepper, and spices as needed.

Serving Suggestions:
Serve hot, topped with a dollop of Greek yogurt or a sprinkle of toasted pumpkin seeds for added texture and protein.

Accompany with a slice of whole-grain bread for a filling meal.

SOUP AND STEW

Pumpkin and Sweet Potato Soup

 SERVES 4   **PREP TIME** 15 MIN.   **COOK TIME** 30 MIN.

Ingredients:

2 cups pumpkin puree
(fresh or canned, unsweetened)
1 large sweet potato
1 medium onion
2 cloves garlic
1 tablespoon olive oil
4 cups low-sodium vegetable broth
1 teaspoon ground cinnamon
1/2 teaspoon ground nutmeg
1/2 teaspoon ground ginger
Salt and pepper to taste

Nutritional Information (Per Serving):

Calories: 180

Protein: 3g

Carbohydrates: 35g

Fats: 4g

Fiber: 6g

Cholesterol: 0mg

Sodium: 300mg

Potassium: 600mg

Directions:

eel and cube the sweet potato. Dice the onion and mince the garlic.

Heat the olive oil over medium heat in a large pot. Add the diced onion and sauté until it becomes translucent, about 5 minutes. Add the minced garlic and sauté for an additional minute until fragrant.

Add the cubed sweet potato to the pot and stir to combine with the onion and garlic.

Stir in the pumpkin puree, ground cinnamon, ground nutmeg, and ground ginger. Mix well to combine all the ingredients.

Pour in the vegetable broth. Bring the mixture to a boil, then reduce the heat to low and simmer for about 20-25 minutes or until the sweet potato is tender.

Use an immersion blender to puree the soup directly in the pot until smooth. Alternatively, carefully transfer the soup in batches to a blender and blend until soft, then return to the pot.

Taste and adjust the seasoning with salt and pepper.

Serving Suggestions:

Serve with whole-grain bread or a green salad for a complete meal.

Top with a dollop of Greek yogurt or a sprinkle of toasted pumpkin seeds for added texture and protein.

Zucchini and Leek Soup

 SERVES 4   **PREP TIME** 15 MIN.   **COOK TIME** 25 MIN.

Ingredients:

3 medium zucchinis
2 leeks, white and light green parts only
1 medium onion
2 cloves garlic
1 tablespoon olive oil
4 cups low-sodium vegetable broth
1 teaspoon dried thyme
Salt and pepper to taste

Nutritional Information (Per Serving):

Calories: 110

Protein: 3g

Carbohydrates: 15g

Fats: 4g

Fiber: 3g

Cholesterol: 0mg

Sodium: 300mg

Potassium: 480mg

Directions:

Zucchinis: Wash and chop into even pieces.

Leeks: Slice the white and light green parts, ensuring they are well cleaned to remove any grit.

Onion and Garlic: Peel, dice the onion, and mince the garlic.

Sauté Vegetables: Heat the olive oil over medium heat in a large pot. Add the onion, leeks, and sauté until they soften, about 5 minutes. Add the garlic and cook for another minute until fragrant.

Add the chopped zucchini to the pot and sauté for a few minutes until they soften.

Pour in the vegetable broth and bring the mixture to a boil. Reduce heat to low, add dried thyme, and let it simmer for about 15 minutes or until the vegetables are very tender.

Use an immersion blender to puree the soup directly in the pot until smooth.

Taste and adjust the seasoning with salt and pepper. Be mindful of the salt if you are following a liver-friendly diet.

Serving Suggestions:

erve this soup as a light lunch or dinner with a side of whole-grain bread.

Pair with a simple salad dressed with olive oil and vinegar for a complete meal.

SOUP AND STEW

Roasted Red Pepper and Tomato

 SERVES 4   **PREP TIME** 15 MIN.   **COOK TIME** 45 MIN.

Ingredients:
4 large red bell peppers
4 medium tomatoes
1 large onion
2 cloves garlic
2 tablespoons olive oil
4 cups low-sodium vegetable broth
1 teaspoon dried basil
1 teaspoon dried oregano
Salt and pepper to taste

Nutritional Information (Per Serving):
Calories: 140
Protein: 3g
Carbohydrates: 18g
Fats: 7g
Fiber: 5g
Cholesterol: 0mg
Sodium: 200mg

Directions:
Preheat your oven to 400°F (200°C).Cut the red bell peppers and tomatoes into quarters, removing the seeds and stems from the peppers.Arrange the peppers and tomatoes on a baking sheet. Drizzle with one tablespoon of olive oil and toss to coat evenly.Roast in the preheated oven for 25-30 minutes until the vegetables are tender and the edges begin to char.

While the vegetables are roasting, heat the remaining tablespoon of olive oil in a large pot over medium heat.Add the diced onion and sauté until translucent, about 5-7 minutes. Add the minced garlic and cook for 1-2 minutes until fragrant.

Remove the roasted vegetables from the oven and let them cool slightly. If desired, peel the skins from the peppers and tomatoes for a smoother soup.Transfer the roasted vegetables to a blender, adding some vegetable broth to help blend smoothly.Puree the vegetables until smooth.

Pour the vegetable puree back into the pot with the onions and garlic.Add the remaining vegetable broth, dried basil, and dried oregano.Season with salt and pepper to taste.Bring to a simmer and cook for 10 minutes, allowing the flavors to meld.

Ladle the soup into bowls.Garnish with fresh basil leaves and a drizzle of balsamic vinegar if desired.

Vegetable and Quinoa Soup

 SERVES 4   **PREP TIME** 15 MIN.   **COOK TIME** 30 MIN.

Ingredients:
1/2 cup quinoa
1 tablespoon olive oil
1 medium onion
2 cloves garlic
2 medium carrots
2 stalks celery
1 medium zucchini
1 red bell pepper
4 cups low-sodium vegetable broth
1 can (15 oz) diced tomatoes, no salt added
1 teaspoon dried thyme
1 teaspoon dried basil
Salt and pepper to taste
2 cups chopped spinach or kale
Fresh parsley, chopped (for garnish)

Nutritional Information (Per Serving):
Calories: 200
Protein: 8g
Carbohydrates: 35g
Fats: 4g
Fiber: 7g
Cholesterol: 0mg
Sodium: 300mg
Potassium: 700mg

Directions:
In a small saucepan, combine the rinsed quinoa with 1 cup of water. Bring to a boil, then reduce heat to low, cover, and simmer for 15 minutes or until the water is absorbed and the quinoa is tender.

Heat the olive oil in a large pot over medium heat. Add the onion and garlic, sauté until the onion becomes translucent, for about 5 minutes.Add the carrots and celery, and continue to sauté for another 5 minutes.Add the zucchini and red bell pepper, cooking for 5 minutes until slightly softening.

Stir in the cooked quinoa, vegetable broth, and diced tomatoes.Season with thyme, basil, salt, and pepper.Bring the mixture to a boil, then reduce heat and simmer for 10 minutes to allow flavors to meld.

Stir in the spinach or kale during the last 5 minutes of cooking, allowing it to wilt but retain its color and nutrients.

Serving Suggestions:
Serve this hearty soup as a main dish with whole-grain bread or crackers.
Consider topping with grated Parmesan cheese or a spoonful of Greek yogurt for added protein

SOUP AND STEW

Carrot and Ginger Soup

 SERVES 4   **PREP TIME** 15 MIN.   **COOK TIME** 30 MIN.

Ingredients:
1 tablespoon olive oil
1 large onion
4 cups carrots, peeled and diced
(about 6-7 medium carrots)
2 tablespoons fresh ginger
3 cloves garlic
4 cups low-sodium vegetable broth
1 teaspoon ground turmeric
Salt and pepper to taste
Fresh parsley or cilantro for garnish

Nutritional Information (Per Serving):
Calories: 140
Protein: 3g
Carbohydrates: 20g
Fats: 5g
Fiber: 5g
Cholesterol: 0mg
Sodium: 200mg
Potassium: 500mg

Directions:
In a large pot, heat the olive oil over medium heat. Add the chopped onion and sauté until translucent, about 5 minutes. Add the minced garlic and grated ginger, sautéing for another 2 minutes until fragrant.

Add the diced carrots to the pot, stirring to mix with the onions, garlic, and ginger. Cook for about 5 minutes, stirring occasionally.

Pour the vegetable broth into the pot. Add the ground turmeric and season with salt and pepper. Bring the mixture to a boil, then reduce the heat and simmer for about 20 minutes or until the carrots are tender.

An immersion blender will puree the soup directly in the pot until smooth.

Taste the soup and adjust the seasoning with additional salt and pepper if needed.

Ladle the soup into bowls. Garnish with chopped parsley or cilantro. Serve with a wedge of lemon on the side, if desired.

Serving Suggestions:
Serve with a slice of whole-grain bread or a small salad for a complete meal.

Top with a dollop of Greek yogurt or a sprinkle of pumpkin seeds for added protein and texture.

Broccoli Soup

 SERVES 4   **PREP TIME** 10 MIN.   **COOK TIME** 20 MIN.

Ingredients:
1 tablespoon olive oil
1 large onion
2 cloves garlic
4 cups broccoli florets
1 medium potato
4 cups low-sodium vegetable broth
1/2 teaspoon salt
(adjust based on dietary needs)
1/4 teaspoon ground black pepper
Fresh parsley or chives for garnish

Nutritional Information (Per Serving):
Calories: 110
Protein: 4g
Carbohydrates: 15g
Fats: 4g
Fiber: 4g
Cholesterol: 0mg
Sodium: 300mg
Potassium: 450mg

Directions:
In a large pot, heat the olive oil over medium heat. Add the chopped onion and sauté until translucent, about 5 minutes. Add the minced garlic and cook for another minute until fragrant.

Add the broccoli florets and diced potato to the pot. Stir to combine with the onions and garlic. Cook for about 3-5 minutes, stirring occasionally.

Pour the vegetable broth into the pot. Bring the mixture to a boil, then reduce the heat and let it simmer for about 15 minutes or until the broccoli and potatoes are very tender.

An immersion blender will puree the soup directly in the pot until smooth.

Add salt, black pepper, and nutmeg (if using). Adjust the seasonings to taste.

Ladle the soup into bowls and garnish with chopped parsley or chives.

Serving Suggestions:
Serve this broccoli soup with whole-grain bread or a light salad for a balanced meal.

SOUP AND STEW

Minestrone Soup

 SERVES 6   **PREP TIME** 15 MIN.   **COOK TIME** 40 MIN.

Ingredients:
1 tablespoon olive oil
1 large onion
2 cloves garlic
2 medium carrots
2 stalks celery
1 medium zucchini
1 cup green beans, trimmed and cut into
1-inch pieces
4 cups low-sodium vegetable broth
1 can (14.5 oz) diced tomatoes,
no salt added
1 can (15 oz) low-sodium cannellini beans
1 teaspoon dried oregano
1 teaspoon dried basil
1/4 teaspoon black pepper
1/2 cup whole grain pasta (e.g., elbows or shells)
2 cups fresh spinach leaves
Fresh basil or parsley for garnish

Nutritional Information (Per Serving):

Calories: 180

Protein: 8g

Carbohydrates: 30g

Fats: 3g

Fiber: 8g

Cholesterol: 0mg

Sodium: 300mg

Potassium: 600mg

Directions:
In a large pot, heat the olive oil over medium heat.Add the onion and garlic, and sauté until the onion is translucent, about 5 minutes.Add the carrots and celery, and cook for another 5 minutes, stirring occasionally.Add the zucchini and green beans, cooking for an additional 5 minutes.
Stir in the vegetable broth and diced tomatoes with their juice.Add the cannellini beans, oregano, basil, salt (if using), and pepper.Bring the mixture to a boil, then reduce the heat and let it simmer for 15 minutes.
Stir in the pasta and continue to simmer for 10 minutes or until the pasta is tender.
Add the spinach leaves and cook until wilted about 2 minutes.

Serving Suggestions:
Serve with a side of crusty whole-grain bread.
Add a sprinkle of grated Parmesan cheese on top for those who can include more protein in their diet.

Mushroom Barley Soup

 SERVES 6   **PREP TIME** 10 MIN.   **COOK TIME** 1 HOUR

Ingredients:
1 tablespoon olive oil
1 large onion
2 cloves garlic
1 cup carrots
1 cup celery
16 oz fresh mushrooms, sliced
(mix of shiitake, button, and portobello)
1 cup pearl barley
6 cups low-sodium vegetable broth
2 teaspoons dried thyme
1 teaspoon dried rosemary
Salt and black pepper to taste
Fresh parsley, chopped (for garnish)

Nutritional Information (Per Serving):

Calories: 200

Protein: 6g

Carbohydrates: 40g

Fats: 3g

Fiber: 9g

Cholesterol: 0mg

Sodium: 200mg

Potassium: 600mg

Directions:
Heat the olive oil in a large pot over medium heat.Add the onion and garlic, and sauté until the onion becomes translucent, about 5 minutes.
Add the carrots and celery, and continue to sauté for about 5 minutes until slightly softened.Stir in the sliced mushrooms and cook for 10 minutes, allowing the mushrooms to release their moisture and brown slightly.
Stir in the rinsed barley, coating it with the mixture in the pot.Pour in the vegetable broth. Bring the mixture to a boil.
Add the dried thyme, rosemary, salt, and black pepper.Reduce heat to low, cover, and let simmer for about 40 minutes or until the barley is fully cooked and tender.

Serving Suggestions:
Pair this hearty soup with a side salad for a balanced meal. For additional protein, consider adding a can of drained and rinsed white beans during the last 10 minutes of cooking.

SOUP AND STEW

Tomato Basil Soup

 SERVES 4   **PREP TIME** 10 MIN.   **COOK TIME** 30 MIN.

Ingredients:
1 tablespoon olive oil
1 large onion
2 cloves garlic
4 cups fresh tomatoes
2 tablespoons tomato paste
4 cups low-sodium vegetable broth
1/2 cup fresh basil leaves
1 teaspoon dried oregano
Salt and pepper to taste

Nutritional Information (Per Serving):

Calories: 100

Protein: 3g

Carbohydrates: 15g

Fats: 3.5g

Fiber: 4g

Cholesterol: 0mg

Sodium: 200mg

Potassium: 600mg

Directions:
Heat the olive oil in a large pot over medium heat.Add the onion and garlic, sauté until the onion is translucent and the garlic is fragrant, about 5 minutes.

Stir in the chopped tomatoes and tomato paste. Cook for 10 minutes until the tomatoes break down and release their juices.

Add chopped fresh basil and dried oregano to the vegetable broth.Season with salt and pepper to taste.Bring to a boil, then reduce heat and simmer for 15 minutes.

Use an immersion blender to purée the soup directly in the pot until smooth.

Serving Suggestions:
Serve this tomato basil soup with whole-grain toast or a small salad for a complete meal.

Add a spoonful of Greek yogurt or sprinkle some grated Parmesan cheese on top for those wanting to increase protein intake.

Lentil and Vegetable Soup

 SERVES 6   **PREP TIME** 15 MIN.   **COOK TIME** 45 MIN.

Ingredients:
1 tablespoon olive oil
1 large onion
2 cloves garlic
2 medium carrots
2 stalks celery
1 red bell pepper
1 cup dried lentils
6 cups low-sodium vegetable broth
1 can (14.5 oz) diced tomatoes, no salt added
1 teaspoon dried thyme
1 teaspoon dried basil
1/2 teaspoon black pepper
2 cups chopped kale or spinach
1 tablespoon lemon juice
Fresh parsley, chopped (for garnish)

Nutritional Information (Per Serving):

Calories: 220

Protein: 12g

Carbohydrates: 35g

Fats: 4g

Fiber: 14g

Cholesterol: 0mg

Sodium: 300mg

Potassium: 600mg

Directions:
In a large pot, heat the olive oil over medium heat.Add the onion and garlic, and sauté until the onion is translucent, about 5 minutes.

Stir in the carrots, celery, and red bell pepper. Cook for about 10 minutes, stirring occasionally, until the vegetables soften. Add the rinsed lentils to the pot, mixing them with the vegetables.Pour in the vegetable broth and add the diced tomatoes with their juice.

Stir in thyme, basil, and black pepper. Bring the mixture to a boil.Reduce the heat to low, cover, and simmer for 25-30 minutes or until the lentils are tender.

Add the chopped kale or spinach during the last 5 minutes of cooking, allowing it to wilt.If needed, stir in the lemon juice and adjust the salt to taste.

Serving Suggestions:
Serve this hearty soup with a slice of whole-grain bread or a side salad.

Consider adding a boiled egg or a sprinkle of grated cheese, if not vegan, for additional protein.

SOUP AND STEW

Thai Coconut Fish Soup

 SERVES 4 **PREP TIME** 15 MIN. **COOK TIME** 20 MIN.

Ingredients:
1 tablespoon olive oil
1 small onion
2 cloves garlic
1 tablespoon fresh ginger
1 red bell pepper
1 medium carrot
2 tablespoons red curry paste
(adjust based on your preference for heat)
4 cups low-sodium vegetable broth
1 can (14 oz) light coconut milk
1 pound firm white fish (like cod or halibut),cut into bite-sized pieces
1 tablespoon lime juice
1/2 cup fresh cilantro

> **Nutritional Information (Per Serving):**
> Calories: 250
> Protein: 22g
> Carbohydrates: 12g
> Fats: 12g
> Fiber: 2g
> Cholesterol: 45mg
> Sodium: 400mg (can be adjusted based on fish sauce use)
> Potassium: 600mg

Directions:
Chop all vegetables and ginger as indicated. Cut the fish into bite-sized pieces.

Heat olive oil in a large pot over medium heat.Add onion, garlic, and ginger, sautéing until the onion becomes translucent, about 5 minutes.Add the red bell pepper and carrot, cooking until slightly softened, about 3 minutes.

Stir in the red curry paste and cook for 1 minute until fragrant.

Pour in the vegetable broth and light coconut milk. Bring to a simmer.

Gently add the fish pieces to the simmering soup. Let cook for about 5-7 minutes or until the fish is opaque and cooked through.

Stir in fish sauce (if using), lime juice, and brown sugar (if using). Adjust these ingredients according to your taste and dietary needs.

Serving Suggestions:
For those managing their carbohydrate intake, serve this soup as a light main course with a side of steamed jasmine or cauliflower rice.

A side of sliced cucumbers in vinegar can complement the flavors nicely.

Cauliflower and Chickpea Stew

 SERVES 4 **PREP TIME** 15 MIN. **COOK TIME** 30 MIN.

Ingredients:
1 tablespoon olive oil
1 large onion
2 cloves garlic
1 head cauliflower
1 can (15 oz) chickpeas
1 can (14.5 oz) diced tomatoes, no salt added
3 cups low-sodium vegetable broth
1 teaspoon ground cumin
1 teaspoon ground coriander
1/2 teaspoon turmeric
1/2 teaspoon paprika
Salt and pepper to taste
1/4 cup chopped fresh cilantro or parsley (for garnish)
Juice of 1 lemon

> **Nutritional Information (Per Serving):**
> Calories: 200
> Protein: 9g
> Carbohydrates: 30g
> Fats: 5g
> Fiber: 8g
> Cholesterol: 0mg
> Sodium: 300mg
> Potassium: 600mg

Directions:
Heat olive oil in a large pot over medium heat.Add the diced onion and cook until soft and translucent, about 5 minutes. Add the minced garlic and cook for an additional minute until fragrant.

Stir in the cauliflower florets and chickpeas. Cook for about 5 minutes, stirring occasionally.

Add the diced tomatoes with their juice, vegetable broth, cumin, coriander, turmeric, and paprika.Bring the mixture to a boil, then reduce the heat to low and let it simmer for about 20 minutes or until the cauliflower is tender.Season with salt and pepper to taste.

Just before serving, stir in the fresh lemon juice.Garnish with chopped cilantro or parsley.

Serving Suggestions:
Serve this hearty Stew with a side of whole-grain bread or over a bed of cooked quinoa for extra protein.

A side salad of mixed greens could complement the Stew for a balanced meal.

SOUP AND STEW

Turkey and Vegetable Stew

 SERVES 6   **PREP TIME** 15 MIN.   **COOK TIME** 45 MIN.

Ingredients:
1 tablespoon olive oil
1 lb ground turkey breast (lean)
1 large onion
2 cloves garlic
2 carrots
2 celery stalks
1 bell pepper
1 zucchini
1 sweet potato
4 cups low-sodium chicken or vegetable broth
1 can (14.5 oz) diced tomatoes, no salt added
1 teaspoon dried thyme
1 teaspoon dried oregano
Salt and pepper to taste
Fresh parsley, chopped (for garnish)

Nutritional Information (Per Serving):
Calories: 250
Protein: 21g
Carbohydrates: 27g
Fats: 7g
Fiber: 6g
Cholesterol: 45mg
Sodium: 300mg
Potassium: 700mg

Directions:
Heat the olive oil in a large pot over medium heat.Add the ground turkey and cook until browned, breaking it up as it cooks, about 5-7 minutes.Remove the turkey and set aside.
Add the onion, garlic, carrots, celery, and bell pepper to the same pot.Cook over medium heat until the vegetables soften, about 8 minutes.
Return the browned turkey to the pot.Add the zucchini, sweet potato, broth, diced tomatoes, thyme, and oregano.
Bring the mixture to a boil, then reduce the heat and let it simmer, covered, for about 30 minutes or until the vegetables and turkey are very tender.Season with salt and pepper to taste. If using, stir in apple cider vinegar for a slight tangy flavor.

Serving Suggestions:
Serve this hearty Stew with a side of whole-grain bread or over a small serving of brown rice or quinoa for added fiber. A crisp green salad would complement the Stew well.

Coconut Curry Vegetable Stew

 SERVES 6   **PREP TIME** 15 MIN.   **COOK TIME** 30 MIN.

Ingredients:
1 tablespoon olive oil
1 large onion
3 cloves garlic
1 tablespoon fresh ginger
1 tablespoon curry powder (adjust based on your preference for heat)
1 teaspoon turmeric
1 medium sweet potato
1 red bell pepper
1 zucchini
1 cup cauliflower florets
1 cup chopped green beans
1 can (14 oz) light coconut milk
4 cups low-sodium vegetable broth
Fresh cilantro or basil for garnish

Nutritional Information (Per Serving):
Calories: 180
Protein: 4g
Carbohydrates: 23g
Fats: 8g
Fiber: 6g
Cholesterol: 0mg
Sodium: 200mg
Potassium: 500mg

Directions:
Heat the olive oil in a large pot over medium heat.Add the onion, garlic, ginger, and sauté until the onion is translucent, about 5 minutes.Stir in the curry powder and turmeric, cooking until fragrant.
Add the sweet potato, red bell pepper, zucchini, cauliflower, and green beans.
Pour in the light coconut milk and vegetable broth. Bring the mixture to a boil.Reduce the heat to low, cover, and simmer for about 20 minutes or until the vegetables are tender.
Season with salt and pepper to taste.Add lime juice for additional flavor if desired.

Serving Suggestions:
Serve this hearty Stew with brown rice or quinoa for a complete meal.
Pair with a simple green salad dressed with lemon vinaigrette.

SOUP AND STEW

Beet and Lentil Stew

 SERVES 6 **PREP TIME** 15 MIN. **COOK TIME** 45 MIN.

Ingredients:
1 tablespoon olive oil
1 large onion,
2 cloves garlic
3 medium beets
2 carrots, peeled and diced
1 cup dried green or brown lentils
4 cups low-sodium vegetable broth
2 cups water
1 teaspoon dried thyme
1 bay leaf
Salt and pepper to taste
2 tablespoons apple cider vinegar
Fresh parsley, chopped (for garnish)

Nutritional Information (Per Serving):

Calories: 200

Protein: 10g

Carbohydrates: 35g

Fats: 3g

Fiber: 10g

Cholesterol: 0mg

Sodium: 200mg

Potassium: 600mg

Directions:
Sauté Aromatics:
In a large pot, heat the olive oil over medium heat.
Add the onion and garlic, sauté until the onion is translucent, about 5 minutes.
Stir in the diced beets and carrots, cooking for about 10 minutes until slightly softened.Add the rinsed lentils to the pot, mixing them with the vegetables.
Pour in the vegetable broth and water. Add the dried thyme and bay leaf.Bring the mixture to a boil, then reduce the heat to low, cover, and simmer for about 30 minutes or until the lentils and beets are tender.Season with salt and pepper to taste.
Stir in the apple cider vinegar towards the end of cooking to brighten the flavors.
Remove the bay leaf.Ladle the Stew into bowls and garnish with fresh parsley.

Serving Suggestions:
Serve this hearty Stew with whole-grain bread or a simple green salad.
For additional protein, top with a dollop of Greek yogurt or sprinkle with feta cheese.

Creamy Broccoli, Carrot, and Turkey Stew

 SERVES 6 **PREP TIME** 15 MIN. **COOK TIME** 30 MIN.

Ingredients:
1 tablespoon olive oil
1 lb ground turkey breast (lean)
1 large onion
2 cloves garlic
2 large carrots
3 cups broccoli florets
4 cups low-sodium chicken broth
1 cup low-fat milk or unsweetened almond milk
2 tablespoons whole wheat flour (or a gluten-free alternative like oat flour)
1 teaspoon dried thyme
Salt and pepper to taste
Fresh parsley, chopped (for garnish)

Nutritional Information (Per Serving):

Calories: 220

Protein: 23g

Carbohydrates: 15g

Fats: 8g

Fiber: 3g

Cholesterol: 55mg

Sodium: 300mg

Potassium: 550mg

Directions:
Heat olive oil in a large pot over medium heat.Add the diced
Heat the olive oil in a large pot over medium heat.Add the ground turkey and cook until browned, breaking it up with a spoon as it cooks, about 5-7 minutes. Remove the turkey from the pot and set aside.
Add the onion and garlic to the same pot and cook until the onion becomes translucent, about 5 minutes.Add the diced carrots and cook for an additional 5 minutes until they start to soften.
Sprinkle the flour over the vegetables and stir well to coat. Cook for about 2 minutes, stirring continuously, to remove the raw flour taste.
Gradually add the chicken broth, stirring continuously to avoid lumps.Return the browned turkey to the pot.Bring to a simmer and cook for 10 minutes or until the carrots are nearly tender.
Add the broccoli florets to the pot.Pour in the milk and stir to combine.Cook for an additional 10 minutes until the broccoli is tender and the Stew has thickened slightly.Season with dried thyme, salt, and pepper to taste.

Serving Suggestions:
Serve with a side of whole-grain bread or a fresh green salad.
For those not on a strict low-fat diet, consider a sprinkle of grated low-fat cheese on top.

SOUP AND STEW

Moroccan Chickpea Stew

 SERVES 6   **PREP TIME** 15 MIN.   **COOK TIME** 45 MIN.

Ingredients:
1 tablespoon olive oil
1 large onion
3 cloves garlic
2 carrots, peeled and diced
2 celery stalks
1 red bell pepper
1 sweet potato
2 teaspoons ground cumin
1 teaspoon ground coriander
1/2 teaspoon ground cinnamon
1/2 teaspoon paprika
1 can (15 oz) chickpeas
1 can (14.5 oz) diced tomatoes, no salt added
4 cups low-sodium vegetable broth
Salt and pepper to taste
Fresh cilantro
1 lemon, cut into wedges (for serving)

Nutritional Information (Per Serving):

Calories: 220

Protein: 8g

Carbohydrates: 40g

Fats: 4g

Fiber: 9g

Cholesterol: 0mg

Sodium: 300mg

Potassium: 750mg

Directions:
In a large pot, heat the olive oil over medium heat. Add the onion and garlic, sauté until the onion is translucent, about 5 minutes. Add the carrots, celery, and red bell pepper, and continue to sauté for another 5 minutes.
Stir in the cumin, coriander, cinnamon, paprika, and cayenne pepper, cooking for 1 minute until fragrant. Add the sweet potato and cook for a few minutes, stirring to coat the vegetables in the spices.
Add the chickpeas and diced tomatoes with their juices. Pour in the vegetable broth and bring the Stew to a boil. Reduce heat to low, cover, and simmer for 30 minutes or until the sweet potatoes are tender.

Serving Suggestions:
Serve this Stew as a hearty meal or alongside whole-grain couscous or quinoa for added texture and protein.
A simple side salad of mixed greens complements the Stew perfectly.

Cauliflower Rice and Chickpea Stew

 SERVES 4 **PREP TIME** 15 MIN.   **COOK TIME** 30 MIN.

Ingredients:
1 tablespoon olive oil
1 large onion
3 cloves garlic
1 tablespoon fresh ginger
1 red bell pepper
1 zucchini
1 can (15 oz) chickpeas
1 can (14.5 oz) diced tomatoes, no salt added
1 teaspoon ground cumin
1 teaspoon ground turmeric
1/2 teaspoon smoked paprika
4 cups riced cauliflower (fresh or frozen)
3 cups low-sodium vegetable broth
Fresh cilantro
1 lemon, cut into wedges (for serving)

Nutritional Information (Per Serving):

Calories: 210

Protein: 9g

Carbohydrates: 35g

Fats: 5g

Fiber: 11g

Cholesterol: 0mg

Sodium: 300mg

Potassium: 800mg

Directions:
Heat the olive oil in a large pot over medium heat. Add the onion and garlic, sauté until the onion is translucent, about 5 minutes. Stir in the grated ginger and cook for another minute.
Add the red bell pepper and zucchini to the pot. Cook for about 5 minutes until they start to soften. Stir in the chickpeas, diced tomatoes, cumin, turmeric, smoked paprika, and cayenne pepper. Mix well to combine the flavors.
Stir in the riced cauliflower and mix thoroughly with the vegetable and spice mixture.
Pour in the vegetable broth and bring the mixture to a simmer. Reduce heat to low, cover, and let it simmer for about 20 minutes, allowing the flavors to meld and the vegetables to become tender.

Serving Suggestions:
This Stew can be a complete meal, providing a balanced mix of proteins, fibers, and nutrients. This Stew pairs well with whole-grain pita bread

SOUP AND STEW

Chicken Liver Vegetable Stew

 SERVES 4   **PREP TIME** 20 MIN.   **COOK TIME** 30 MIN.

Ingredients:
1 tablespoon olive oil
1 pound chicken livers
1 large onion
2 cloves garlic
2 carrots
2 celery stalks
1 bell pepper
1 zucchini
4 cups low-sodium chicken broth
1 can (14.5 oz) diced tomatoes, no salt added
1 teaspoon dried thyme
1 teaspoon dried rosemary
Salt and pepper to taste
Fresh parsley

Nutritional Information (Per Serving):
Calories: 280
Protein: 26g
Carbohydrates: 15g
Fats: 12g
Fiber: 3g
Cholesterol: 300mg
Sodium: 300mg
Potassium: 800mg

Directions:
Rinse the chicken livers under cold water, pat dry, and trim any fat or connective tissue. Halve them to ensure even cooking.
Heat the olive oil in a large pot over medium-high heat.Add the chicken livers and sauté until they are browned on all sides, about 3-5 minutes. Remove them from the pot and set aside.
In the same pot, reduce the heat to medium. Add the onion and garlic, sauté until the onion is translucent, about 5 minutes.Add the carrots, celery, bell pepper, and zucchini. Cook, stirring occasionally, until the vegetables soften, about 5 minutes.
Return the chicken livers to the pot. Add the diced tomatoes and chicken broth.Stir in the thyme and rosemary.Bring the Stew to a boil, then reduce the heat to low and simmer, covered, for about 20 minutes.

Serving Suggestions:
Serve this Stew with steamed green beans or a mixed green salad for a well-rounded meal.
Pair with cauliflower rice instead of traditional rice for those managing carbohydrate intake.

Moroccan Spiced Fish Stew

 SERVES 4   **PREP TIME** 15 MIN.   **COOK TIME** 25 MIN.

Ingredients:
 tablespoon olive oil
1 large onion
3 cloves garlic
1 red bell pepper
2 medium carrots
2 teaspoons ground cumin
1 teaspoon ground coriander
1/2 teaspoon ground cinnamon
1/2 teaspoon paprika
1 can (14.5 oz) diced tomatoes, no salt added
4 cups low-sodium vegetable broth
1 pound firm white fish (like cod or halibut), cut into chunks
1 cup chopped fresh cilantro
Salt and pepper to taste
Juice of 1 lemon

Nutritional Information (Per Serving):
Calories: 220
Protein: 23g
Carbohydrates: 18g
Fats: 7g
Fiber: 4g
Cholesterol: 55mg
Sodium: 300mg
Potassium: 750mg

Directions:
In a large pot, heat the olive oil over medium heat.Add the onion and garlic, and sauté until the onion is translucent, about 5 minutes.Add the red bell pepper and carrots, sautéing for another 5 minutes until they soften.
Stir in cumin, coriander, cinnamon, paprika, and cayenne pepper. Cook for 1 minute until fragrant.
Add the diced tomatoes, their juices, and vegetable broth to the pot. Bring the mixture to a simmer.
Gently add the fish chunks to the pot. Simmer gently for 10-15 minutes or until the fish is cooked and flakes easily with a fork.
Stir in the chopped cilantro and lemon juice, season with salt and pepper to taste.

Serving Suggestions:
Serve this flavorful Stew with whole-grain couscous or quinoa to absorb the delicious juices and add fiber.
A side salad of arugula or mixed greens would complement the spices well.

SOUP AND STEW

Apple Chicken Stew

 SERVES 4   **PREP TIME** 20 MIN.   **COOK TIME** 45 MIN.

Ingredients:
1 tablespoon olive oil
1 lb chicken breast
1 large onion
2 cloves garlic
2 medium apples (choose a firm variety like Granny Smith or Honeycrisp)
2 large carrots
2 celery stalks
1 teaspoon dried thyme
1/2 teaspoon ground cinnamon
4 cups low-sodium chicken broth
1 bay leaf
Salt and pepper to taste
Fresh parsley

Nutritional Information (Per Serving):

Calories: 275

Protein: 26g

Carbohydrates: 22g

Fats: 8g

Fiber: 4g

Cholesterol: 65mg

Sodium: 200mg

Potassium: 600mg

Directions:
Heat the olive oil in a large pot over medium heat.Add the chicken pieces and cook until browned on all sides, about 5-7 minutes. Remove the chicken from the pot and set aside.
Add the onion and garlic to the same pot. Sauté until the onion becomes translucent, about 5 minutes.
Stir in the apples, carrots, and celery. Cook for about 10 minutes, stirring occasionally, until the vegetables soften.
Return the chicken to the pot. Add the thyme, cinnamon, chicken broth, and bay leaf. Bring to a boil.Reduce the heat to low and simmer, covered, for about 30 minutes, or until the chicken is tender and the flavors are well blended.Season with salt and pepper to taste.
Discard the bay leaf.Garnish with fresh parsley before serving.

Serving Suggestions:
Serve this Stew with a side of whole-grain bread or over a bed of cooked quinoa for added fiber.
A simple green salad with a light vinaigrette dressing would complement the Stew nicely.

Southwest Turkey Stew

 SERVES 6   **PREP TIME** 15 MIN.   **COOK TIME** 45 MIN.

Ingredients:
1 tablespoon olive oil
1 pound ground turkey breast (lean)
1 large onion
3 cloves garlic
1 red bell pepper
1 green bell pepper
2 cups diced tomatoes
 (fresh or no salt added canned)
1 can (15 oz) black beans
1 can (15 oz) corn, no salt added, drained (or 1.5 cups frozen corn)
4 cups low-sodium chicken broth
2 teaspoons chili powder
1 teaspoon cumin
1/2 teaspoon smoked paprika
Salt and black pepper to taste
Fresh cilantro
Juice of one lime

Nutritional Information (Per Serving):

Calories: 250

Protein: 23g

Carbohydrates: 28g

Fats: 6g

Fiber: 6g

Cholesterol: 45mg

Sodium: 300mg

Potassium: 650mg

Directions:
Heat the olive oil in a large pot over medium heat.Add the ground turkey and cook until it is browned and crumbled, about 8-10 minutes. Remove the turkey from the pot and set aside.
Add the onion, garlic, red bell pepper, and green bell pepper in the same pot. Sauté until the vegetables are softened, about 5 minutes.
Return the browned turkey to the pot. Add the diced tomatoes, black beans, and corn.Pour the chicken broth, then stir in the chili powder, cumin, and smoked paprika.
Bring the mixture to a boil, then reduce the heat and let it simmer for about 30 minutes, allowing the flavors to meld together.
Season with salt and black pepper to taste. Stir in the lime juice just before serving.

Serving Suggestions:
Serve this hearty Stew with a side of whole-grain tortillas or over a small serving of brown rice to add more fiber.
A simple side salad with leafy greens can add freshness and balance.

SOUP AND STEW

Spring-Thyme Chicken Stew Soup

 SERVES 6   **PREP TIME** 20 MIN.   **COOK TIME** 35 MIN.

Ingredients:
1 tablespoon olive oil
1.5 pounds of chicken breast cut into bite-sized pieces
1 large onion
3 cloves garlic
3 carrots
2 stalks celery
1 cup fresh peas (or frozen if out of season)
1 cup asparagus, cut into 1-inch pieces
4 cups low-sodium chicken broth
2 teaspoons fresh thyme, chopped (or 1 tsp dried thyme)
Salt and pepper to taste
Juice of 1 lemon
2 tablespoons fresh parsley

Nutritional Information (Per Serving):

Calories: 230

Protein: 28g

Carbohydrates: 15g

Fats: 6g

Fiber: 4g

Cholesterol: 65mg

Sodium: 200mg

Potassium: 600mg

Directions:
Heat the olive oil in a large pot over medium heat.Add the chicken pieces and season with a bit of salt and pepper. Cook until lightly browned and nearly cooked through, about 5-7 minutes. Remove from the pot and set aside.

In the same pot, add the onion and garlic and sauté until the onion is translucent, for about 5 minutes.Add the carrots and celery, continuing to cook until they start to soften, about five more minutes.

Sprinkle the whole wheat flour over the vegetables and stir to coat. Cook for a minute to remove the raw flour taste.

Slowly pour in the chicken broth, stirring constantly to avoid lumps.Return the chicken to the pot, add the fresh or dried thyme, and bring to a simmer.Let simmer for 15 minutes.

Add the fresh peas and asparagus, cooking for 10 minutes or until the vegetables are tender and the chicken is fully cooked.

Stir in the lemon juice and adjust the salt and pepper to taste.

Serving Suggestions:
Serve this light, flavorful Stew with a side of whole-grain bread or over a small serving of cooked quinoa for added fiber. A simple green salad with olive oil and vinegar complements this meal nicely.

LUNCH

Grilled Lemon Herb Chicken Salad

 SERVES 4   **PREP TIME** 20 MIN.   **COOK TIME** 10 MIN.

Ingredients:
For the Chicken:
4 boneless, skinless chicken breasts
2 cloves garlic
Juice of 2 lemons
1 tablespoon olive oil
1 teaspoon dried oregano
1 teaspoon dried thyme
For the Salad:
4 cups mixed salad greens
(spinach, arugula, romaine)
1 cup cherry tomatoes
1 cucumber
1/4 red onion
1 carrot, shredded
1 bell pepper
For the Dressing:
Juice of 1 lemon
2 tablespoons balsamic vinegar
1 tablespoon Dijon mustard
2 tablespoons olive oil
Fresh herbs

Nutritional Information (Per Serving):
Calories: 290
Protein: 28 g
Carbohydrates: 18 g
Fats: 12 g
Fiber: 4 g
Cholesterol: 65 mg
Sodium: 200 mg
Potassium: 600 mg

Directions:
Combine lemon juice, olive oil, minced garlic, oregano, thyme, salt, and pepper in a bowl. Add the chicken breasts, ensuring they are well-coated with the marinade. Let them marinate for at least 15 minutes, preferably in the refrigerator.Preheat the grill to medium-high heat. Remove the chicken from the marinade and grill for about 5 minutes on each side, or until it is thoroughly cooked and has an internal temperature of 165°F (75°C). Remove from the grill and let rest for a few minutes before slicing thinly.Combine salad greens, cherry tomatoes, cucumber, red onion, carrot, and bell pepper in a large bowl. Whisk together lemon juice, balsamic vinegar, Dijon mustard, and honey in a small bowl. Gradually whisk in olive oil until the dressing is emulsified. Add the grilled chicken slices to the salad. Drizzle the dressing over the salad and toss gently to combine. Sprinkle with fresh herbs if using.

Serving Suggestions:
This salad is best enjoyed fresh, but leftovers can be stored in an airtight container in the refrigerator for up to a day. Pair with a whole-grain roll or a small serving of quinoa for an extra fiber boost.

Quinoa and Black Bean Stuffed Bell Peppers

 SERVES 4   **PREP TIME** 20 MIN.   **COOK TIME** 30 MIN.

Ingredients:
4 large bell peppers (any color), tops cut away and seeds removed
1 cup quinoa
2 cups low-sodium vegetable broth
1 can (15 oz) black beans
1 cup corn kernels
1 small onion
2 cloves garlic
1 teaspoon cumin
1/2 teaspoon chili powder
1/4 cup chopped fresh cilantro
Juice of 1 lime
1 tablespoon olive oil

Nutritional Information (Per Serving):
Calories: 350
Protein: 15 g
Carbohydrates: 55 g
Fats: 8 g
Fiber: 12 g
Sodium: 300 mg
Potassium: 800 mg

Directions:
In a medium saucepan, bring the vegetable broth to a boil. Add the rinsed quinoa, reduce heat to low, cover, and simmer for about 15-20 minutes, or until the broth is absorbed and the quinoa is tender.
While the quinoa is cooking, heat olive oil in a skillet over medium heat. Add the onion and garlic, sautéing until the onion is translucent, about 5 minutes.Stir in the black beans, corn, cumin, and chili powder. Cook for another 5 minutes until the vegetables are heated through.Remove from heat and stir in the cooked quinoa, cilantro, and lime juice. Season with salt and pepper to taste.
Preheat your oven to 375°F (190°C).Pack each bell pepper with the quinoa and black bean mixture tightly.Top with shredded cheese if using.Place the stuffed peppers upright in a baking dish.
Cover the dish with foil and bake in the oven for 25-30 minutes, or until the peppers are tender and the filling is hot. Remove the foil in the last 5 minutes if you want the cheese to brown.

Serving Suggestions:
Enjoy these stuffed peppers with a side salad dressed with a vinaigrette for a complete meal.

LUNCH

Turkey and Avocado Wrap

 SERVES 4   **PREP TIME** 15 MIN.   **COOK TIME** 15 MIN.

Ingredients:
4 whole-grain tortillas
8 ounces sliced turkey breast
1 ripe avocado
2 cups mixed greens
(such as spinach, arugula, and romaine)
1 medium carrot
1/2 cucumber
1/4 red onion
4 tablespoons hummus (low-fat)
1 tablespoon lemon juice
1 teaspoon olive oil

Nutritional Information (Per Serving):

Calories: 320

Protein: 22 g

Carbohydrates: 36 g

Fats: 12 g

Fiber: 9 g

Cholesterol: 30 mg

Sodium: 400 mg

Potassium: 600 mg

Directions:
In a small bowl, mix the lemon juice and olive oil. Toss the mixed greens, shredded carrot, cucumber, and red onion in this dressing to lightly coat. Season with a little salt and pepper if desired.
Lay out the whole-grain tortillas on a clean surface.Spread 1 tablespoon of hummus on each tortilla.Divide the turkey slices evenly among the tortillas, placing them over the hummus.Add the dressed vegetables to each tortilla.Top with avocado slices. If desired, sprinkle a bit of chili flakes or paprika over the avocado for extra flavor.
Fold in the sides of the tortilla and roll tightly to enclose the filling.Cut each wrap in half diagonally.

Serving Suggestions:
Enjoy these stuffed peppers with a side salad dressed with a vinaigrette for a complete meal.

Spinach and Feta Stuffed Portobello Mushrooms

 SERVES 4   **PREP TIME** 15 MIN.   **COOK TIME** 20 MIN.

Ingredients:
4 large Portobello mushroom caps
2 teaspoons olive oil
2 cloves garlic
4 cups fresh spinach
1/2 cup crumbled feta cheese (low-fat)
1/4 cup finely chopped red onions
2 tablespoons chopped fresh basil
1 tablespoon balsamic vinegar

Nutritional Information (Per Serving):

Calories: 150

Protein: 8 g

Carbohydrates: 10 g

Fats: 9 g

Fiber: 3 g

Cholesterol: 15 mg

Sodium: 200 mg

Potassium: 400 mg

Directions:
Preheat your oven to 375°F (190°C).
Brush each mushroom cap with olive oil. Place them stem-side up on a baking sheet lined with parchment paper.
Heat a skillet over medium heat. Add the remaining olive oil and minced garlic, sautéing for about 1 minute until fragrant. Add the spinach and cook until it wilts, about 3-4 minutes. Remove from heat.
Combine the wilted spinach, crumbled feta, red onions, and fresh basil in a bowl. Drizzle with balsamic vinegar and mix well. Season with salt and pepper if desired.
Divide the spinach mixture evenly among the mushroom caps, filling each one generously.
Bake in the oven for about 20 minutes or until the mushrooms are tender and the topping is golden.Remove from the oven and sprinkle with pine nuts if using.

Serving Suggestions:
For a complete meal, serve these stuffed mushrooms as a main dish with a side of quinoa or a fresh garden salad.

LUNCH

Lentil and Vegetable Stir-Fry

 SERVES 4   **PREP TIME** 10 MIN.   **COOK TIME** 20 MIN.

Ingredients:
1 cup dry green lentils
3 cups water
1 tablespoon olive oil
1 medium onion
2 cloves garlic
1 bell pepper
2 medium carrots
1 zucchini
1 cup chopped broccoli florets
2 tablespoons low-sodium soy
sauce or tamari
1 tablespoon fresh ginger
1 teaspoon sesame oil

Nutritional Information (Per Serving):
Calories: 280
Protein: 15 g
Carbohydrates: 40 g
Fats: 7 g
Fiber: 16 g
Sodium: 300 mg
Potassium: 710 mg

Directions:
Rinse the lentils under cold water until the water runs clear.In a medium saucepan, bring 3 cups of water to a boil. Add the lentils, reduce heat, cover, and simmer for 15-20 minutes until tender but firm. Drain any excess water and set aside.
Heat the olive oil in a large skillet or wok over medium heat. Add the onion and garlic, and sauté for 2-3 minutes until the onions become translucent.Add the bell pepper, carrots, zucchini, and broccoli to the skillet. Stir-fry for about 5-7 minutes until the vegetables are tender yet crisp.
Add the cooked lentils to the skillet with the vegetables.Stir in the soy sauce, ginger, and sesame oil. Mix well to combine all the ingredients.
Add chili flakes or fresh chili to introduce a spicy element without adding fat if desired.

Serving Suggestions:
Pair it with brown rice or quinoa for a more filling meal or a simple side salad with lemon and olive oil.

Baked Salmon with Asparagus and Cherry Tomatoes

 SERVES 4   **PREP TIME** 10 MIN.   **COOK TIME** 20 MIN.

Ingredients:
4 salmon filets skin on
1 tablespoon olive oil
1 pound asparagus, ends trimmed
1 cup cherry tomatoes, halved
2 cloves garlic, minced
Juice of 1 lemon

Nutritional Information (Per Serving):
Calories: 350
Protein: 15 g
Carbohydrates: 55 g
Fats: 8 g
Fiber: 12 g
Sodium: 300 mg
Potassium: 800 mg

Directions:
Preheat your oven to 400°F (200°C).
On a large baking sheet, arrange the asparagus and scatter the cherry tomatoes around. Drizzle with half the olive oil and sprinkle with minced garlic. Toss to coat.
Place the salmon filets skin-side down on the baking sheet among the vegetables. Drizzle the remaining olive oil over the salmon. Squeeze lemon juice over the salmon and vegetables. Season lightly with salt and pepper if using.
Place the baking sheet in the oven and bake for about 15-20 minutes, or until the salmon is cooked, flakes easily with a fork, and the vegetables are tender.Remove from the oven. Garnish with fresh dill or parsley if desired.

Serving Suggestions:
For an added fiber boost, serve with a side of quinoa or a mixed green salad.

LUNCH

Chickpea and Cucumber Tabbouleh

 SERVES 4   **PREP TIME** 15 MIN.   **COOK TIME** 30 MIN.

Ingredients:
cup cooked chickpeas
1 large cucumber
2 cups fresh parsley
1/2 cup fresh mint
4 green onions
1 cup cherry tomatoes
1/4 cup lemon juice
2 tablespoons olive oil

Nutritional Information (Per Serving):
Calories: 180
Protein: 6 g
Carbohydrates: 20 g
Fats: 9 g
Fiber: 6 g
Sodium: 15 mg
Potassium: 400 mg

Directions:
Finely chop the parsley and mint, slice the green onions, dice the cucumber, and quarter the cherry tomatoes.
Combine chickpeas, cucumber, parsley, mint, green onions, and cherry tomatoes in a large mixing bowl.
In a small bowl, whisk together the lemon juice and olive oil. Pour this dressing over the salad mixture and toss well to coat evenly. Season with salt, pepper, and sumac (if using) to taste.
For the best flavor, cover the salad and refrigerate for at least 30 minutes before serving. This allows the flavors to meld together.

Serving Suggestions:
This tabbouleh can be served alongside grilled chicken or fish for a protein-rich meal.

Grilled Shrimp and Mango Salad

 SERVES 4   **PREP TIME** 15 MIN.   **COOK TIME** 6 MIN.

Ingredients:
20 large shrimp (about 1 pound), peeled and deveined
1 large ripe mango
2 cups mixed greens
1 red bell pepper
1 avocado
1/4 cup red onion
Juice of 2 limes
2 tablespoons olive oil
1 garlic clove

Nutritional Information (Per Serving):
Calories: 290
Protein: 24 g
Carbohydrates: 20 g
Fats: 14 g
Fiber: 5 g
Cholesterol: 180 mg
Sodium: 150 mg
Potassium: 500 mg

Directions:
Preheat your grill to medium-high heat.Mix one tablespoon of olive oil in a small bowl, juice of 1 lime, minced garlic, and a pinch of salt and pepper (if using). Toss the shrimp in this marinade and let sit for 10 minutes.
Thread the shrimp on skewers. Grill for 2-3 minutes per side or until the shrimp are opaque and slightly charred.
Combine the mixed greens, sliced bell pepper, diced mango, sliced avocado, and red onion in a large salad bowl.
Whisk together the remaining one tablespoon of olive oil, juice of 1 lime, and honey (if using) in a small bowl—season with a bit of salt and pepper to taste.
Add the grilled shrimp to the salad. Drizzle with the dressing and toss gently to combine.

Serving Suggestions:
This salad is perfect for a light, refreshing lunch or dinner, especially in warm weather.
Serve with whole-grain bread or a few whole-grain crackers for added fiber.

LUNCH

Zucchini Noodles with Pesto and Cherry Tomatoes

 SERVES 4   **PREP TIME** 10 MIN.   **COOK TIME** 5 MIN.

Ingredients:
4 large zucchinis, spiralized into noodles
1 cup cherry tomatoes
For the Pesto:
1/2 cup fresh basil leaves
1/4 cup pine nuts
2 cloves garlic
2 tablespoons lemon juice
1/4 cup grated Parmesan cheese
1/4 cup olive oil

Nutritional Information (Per Serving):

Calories: 250

Protein: 6 g

Carbohydrates: 10 g

Fats: 21 g

Fiber: 3 g

Sodium: 75 mg

Potassium: 520 mg

Directions:
Combine the basil leaves, pine nuts, garlic, lemon juice, and Parmesan cheese in a food processor. Pulse until coarsely chopped. While the processor runs, slowly pour the olive oil until the mixture forms a smooth paste. Season with salt and pepper if desired.

Heat a large non-stick skillet over medium heat. Add the zucchini noodles and sauté for 2-3 minutes until tender. Be careful not to overcook to avoid them becoming soggy.

Remove the skillet from heat. Add the cherry tomatoes and pesto to the zucchini noodles. Toss gently to combine, ensuring the noodles are evenly coated with the pesto.

Serving Suggestions:
You can top it with grilled chicken or shrimp for added protein.

Greek Yogurt Chicken Salad

 SERVES 4   **PREP TIME** 15 MIN.   **COOK TIME** 30 MIN.

Ingredients:
2 cups cooked chicken breast
1 cup Greek yogurt, low-fat
1/2 cup celery
1/2 cup apple
1/4 cup red onion
1/4 cup walnuts
2 tablespoons lemon juice
1 teaspoon Dijon mustard
1/2 teaspoon dried dill or
1 tablespoon fresh dill

Nutritional Information (Per Serving):

Calories: 180

Protein: 25 g

Carbohydrates: 10 g

Fats: 4 g

Fiber: 2 g

Cholesterol: 60 mg

Sodium: 125 mg

Potassium: 300 mg

Directions:
Use precooked chicken breast, either grilled or poached. Shred the chicken into small pieces.

Combine the shredded chicken, Greek yogurt, celery, apple, red onion, and walnuts in a large bowl. Mix well to ensure an even distribution of the yogurt.

Add the lemon juice, Dijon mustard, dill, and garlic powder if using—season with a bit of salt and pepper to taste. Stir well until all ingredients are thoroughly combined.

Cover the salad and refrigerate for at least 30 minutes to allow the flavors to meld together for best results.

Serving Suggestions:
Serve the chicken salad chilled. It can be served over a bed of mixed greens, wrapped in lettuce leaves for a low-carb option, or as a filling for a whole-grain sandwich.

LUNCH

Curried Cauliflower and Chickpea Bowl

 SERVES 4   **PREP TIME 15 MIN.**   **COOK TIME 30 MIN.**

Ingredients:
20 large shrimp (about 1 pound),
1 large head of cauliflower
1 can (15 oz) chickpeas
1 tablespoon olive oil
2 teaspoons curry powder
1 teaspoon turmeric
1/2 teaspoon cumin
1/4 teaspoon cayenne pepper
1 large onion
2 cloves garlic
1 cup cooked quinoa
1/2 cup coconut milk (light)
4 cups fresh spinach

Nutritional Information (Per Serving):

Calories: 350

Protein: 15 g

Carbohydrates: 45 g

Fats: 12 g

Fiber: 12 g

Sodium: 200 mg

Potassium: 800 mg

Directions:
Preheat your oven to 400°F (200°C).In a large bowl, toss the cauliflower florets and chickpeas with olive oil, curry powder, turmeric, cumin, cayenne pepper, and a pinch of salt.Spread the mixture on a baking sheet and roast for about 20-25 minutes, stirring halfway through, until the cauliflower is tender and golden.

While the cauliflower and chickpeas are roasting, cook the quinoa according to package instructions.

Heat a large skillet over medium heat. Add olive oil, then sauté the onion and garlic until the onion is translucent, about 5-7 minutes.

Add the roasted cauliflower and chickpeas to the skillet with the onions and garlic. Pour in the coconut milk and bring to a simmer. Add the spinach and cook until wilted, about 1-2 minutes.

Spoon the cooked quinoa into bowls. Top with the cauliflower, chickpea, and spinach mixture. Garnish with fresh cilantro.

Serving Suggestions:
This dish is hearty and satisfying on its own but can be accompanied by a side salad for extra greens.

Spinach and Mushrooms Frittata

 SERVES 4   **PREP TIME 10 MIN.**   **COOK TIME 20 MIN.**

Ingredients:
4 large eggs
4 large egg whites
1 cup fresh spinach
1 cup mushrooms
1 medium onion
2 cloves garlic
1/4 cup low-fat milk
1/2 teaspoon dried thyme
1 tablespoon olive oil

Nutritional Information (Per Serving):

Calories: 150

Protein: 12 g

Carbohydrates: 5 g

Fats: 9 g

Fiber: 1 g

Cholesterol: 170 mg

Sodium: 200 mg

Potassium: 300 mg

Directions:
Preheat your oven to 375°F (190°C).

Heat olive oil in a 10-inch oven-safe skillet over medium heat.Add the onion and garlic, and sauté until the onion is translucent, about 3-4 minutes.Add the mushrooms and cook until they are soft, about 5 minutes.Stir in the spinach and cook until just wilted, about 1-2 minutes.

In a bowl, whisk together the eggs, egg whites, low-fat milk, thyme, and optional salt and pepper.If using, stir in the Parmesan cheese.

Pour the egg mixture over the sautéed vegetables in the skillet. Stir gently to ensure the ingredients are evenly distributed.

Transfer the skillet to the oven and bake for 10-15 minutes until the eggs are set and the top is lightly golden.

Serving Suggestions:
This frittata can be served at any meal. It pairs well with a side salad for lunch, dinner, or whole-grain toast for breakfast.

For an added nutrient boost, serve with roasted vegetables or fresh fruit.

LUNCH

Baked Cod with Lemon and Dill

 SERVES 4   **PREP TIME** 10 MIN.   **COOK TIME** 15 MIN.

Ingredients:
4 cod filets
2 tablespoons olive oil
Juice of 1 lemon
1 tablespoon fresh dill
1 lemon

Nutritional Information (Per Serving):

Calories: 190

Protein: 23 g

Carbohydrates: 1 g

Fats: 10 g

Fiber: 0 g

Cholesterol: 55 mg

Sodium: 70 mg

Potassium: 520 mg

Directions:
Preheat your oven to 400°F (200°C).
Rinse the cod filets and pat them dry with paper towels.Place the cod in a baking dish.
In a small bowl, mix together the olive oil, lemon juice, fresh dill, and minced garlic, if using. Season with salt and pepper if desired.Pour this mixture over the cod filets, ensuring they are evenly coated.
Place the lemon slices on top of the cod filets.Bake in the preheated oven for about 12-15 minutes, or until the cod flakes easily with a fork.

Serving Suggestions:
Serve this dish with a side of steamed vegetables like asparagus or green beans and a serving of quinoa or a mixed green salad for a balanced meal.
For added flavor without increasing the fat content, consider serving with a light yogurt-based dill sauce on the side.

Beet and Goat Cheese Salad Boiled

 SERVES 4   **PREP TIME** 10 MIN.   **COOK TIME** 55 MIN.

Ingredients:
4 medium beets
1/2 cup low-fat goat cheese
2 cups arugula or mixed salad greens
1/4 cup walnuts
2 tablespoons balsamic vinegar
1 tablespoon extra-virgin olive oil
 Fresh herbs

Nutritional Information (Per Serving):

Calories: 170

Protein: 6 g

Carbohydrates: 13 g

Fats: 10 g

Fiber: 3 g

Cholesterol: 13 mg

Sodium: 200 mg

Potassium: 400 mg

Directions:
If not using precooked beets, place them in a large pot and cover them with water. Bring to a boil over high heat, then reduce to a simmer and cook until tender, about 45 minutes. Drain, cool, peel, and slice into wedges or cubes.
In a small bowl, whisk together balsamic vinegar and olive oil. Season with a pinch of salt and pepper if desired.
Place the arugula or mixed greens in a large salad bowl. Add the sliced beets on top.Drizzle half of the dressing over the salad and gently toss to combine.
Sprinkle the crumbled goat cheese and optional walnuts over the salad.
For best flavor, cover and refrigerate the salad for about 1 hour before serving.
Drizzle the remaining dressing over the salad just before serving.Garnish with fresh herbs if using.

Serving Suggestions:
This salad serves well as a light lunch or a starter for a more substantial dinner.
Pair with a lean protein like grilled chicken or fish for a balanced meal.

LUNCH

Turkey and Sweet Potato Chili

 SERVES 6   **PREP TIME** 10 MIN.   **COOK TIME** 20 MIN.

Ingredients:
1 lb ground turkey breast
1 large sweet potato
1 large onion
1 red bell pepper
2 cloves garlic
1 can (15 oz) low-sodium black beans
1 can (15 oz) low-sodium diced
 tomatoes with juice
2 tablespoons tomato paste
2 cups low-sodium chicken broth
1 tablespoon chili powder
1 teaspoon ground cumin
1/2 teaspoon paprika
1/4 teaspoon cayenne pepper
1 tablespoon olive oil

Nutritional Information (Per Serving):
Calories: 200
Protein: 15 g
Carbohydrates: 8 g
Fats: 12 g
Fiber: 2 g
Cholesterol: 35 mg
Sodium: 200 mg
Potassium: 500 mg

Directions:
Preheat your oven to 400°F (200°C).Place tomato halves on a baking sheet and cut side up. Drizzle with one tablespoon of olive oil and season lightly with salt and pepper if desired. Roast in the oven for 20 minutes or until the tomatoes are soft and slightly charred.
Whisk together the balsamic vinegar, one tablespoon of olive oil, and Dijon mustard in a small bowl. Set aside.
Combine the arugula, spinach, and red onion in a large salad bowl.Add the roasted tomatoes to the salad.Gently place the sardines on top of the salad.
Drizzle the dressing over the salad. Toss gently to combine, not breaking the sardines too much.
If using, sprinkle capers over the salad for an extra burst of flavor.

Serving Suggestions:
This salad is excellent for a light lunch or a starter for a larger meal.
Pair it with a whole-grain roll or a slice of rustic bread to add fiber and fill it more.

Eggplant and Tomato Stack with Basil

 SERVES 4   **PREP TIME** 20 MIN.   **COOK TIME** 10 MIN.

Ingredients:
2 large eggplants, sliced into
 1/2-inch rounds
4 large ripe tomatoes
1/4 cup fresh basil leaves
2 tablespoons balsamic vinegar
1 tablespoon olive oil

Nutritional Information (Per Serving):
Calories: 120
Protein: 3 g
Carbohydrates: 18 g
Fats: 5 g
Fiber: 9 g
Sodium: 10 mg
Potassium: 700 mg

Directions:
Preheat your grill or a grill pan over medium-high heat.Brush each eggplant slice lightly with olive oil. Grill the eggplant slices for 2-3 minutes per side or until they are tender and have grill marks. Set aside to cool slightly.
On a serving platter, start by placing a slice of grilled eggplant, then a slice of tomato, and a slice of cheese if using. Repeat the layering process until you have built up a few layers, finishing with a slice of eggplant.
Drizzle the balsamic vinegar over the stacks.Scatter fresh basil leaves on top of each stack.
Season with salt and pepper to taste if desired.

Serving Suggestions:
This dish can be served as a light main course or a stunning side dish.
Pair with a protein such as grilled chicken or fish for a balanced meal.

LUNCH

Lemon Garlic Grilled Tuna with Mixed Greens

 SERVES 4   **PREP TIME** 15 MIN.   **COOK TIME** 10 MIN.

Ingredients:
4 tuna steaks
Juice of 1 lemon
2 cloves garlic
2 tablespoons olive oil
1 teaspoon dried thyme
4 cups mixed greens
1 small red onion
1/2 cup cherry tomatoes
1 cucumber

Nutritional Information (Per Serving):
Calories: 280
Protein: 28 g
Carbohydrates: 8 g
Fats: 15 g
Fiber: 3 g
Cholesterol: 50 mg
Sodium: 100 mg
Potassium: 800 mg

Directions:
Combine the lemon juice, olive oil, minced garlic, and thyme in a small bowl. Whisk together until well blended.Place the tuna steaks in a shallow dish and pour the marinade over them, ensuring each piece is well coated. Cover and refrigerate for about 10 minutes.

Preheat an outdoor grill or stovetop grill pan to medium-high heat.

Combine the mixed greens, sliced red onion, cherry tomatoes, and cucumber in a large salad bowl and toss lightly to combine.

Remove the tuna from the marinade, letting the excess drip off. Season with salt and pepper, if desired.Grill the tuna steaks for 4-5 minutes per side or until desired doneness is reached.

Serving Suggestions:
For those who want a more substantial meal, serve with whole-grain bread or a small serving of quinoa.

Avocado Lime Chicken Salad

 SERVES 4   **PREP TIME** 20 MIN.   **COOK TIME** 10 MIN.

Ingredients:
2 large chicken breasts
2 ripe avocados
Juice of 2 limes
1 cup cherry tomatoes
1/2 red onion
1/4 cup cilantro
1 cucumber
1 bell pepper
2 tablespoons olive oil

Nutritional Information (Per Serving):
Calories: 350
Protein: 25 g
Carbohydrates: 15 g
Fats: 22 g
Fiber: 7 g
Cholesterol: 60 mg
Sodium: 150 mg
Potassium: 900 mg

Directions:
Preheat a grill or grill pan over medium-high heat.Season the chicken breasts lightly with salt and pepper if desired. Grill until cooked through, about 5-6 minutes per side. Allow to cool slightly, then shred using two forks.

Combine the diced avocados, lime juice, cherry tomatoes, red onion, cilantro, cucumber, and bell pepper in a large mixing bowl. Toss gently to combine without breaking the avocado pieces.

Add the shredded chicken to the salad mixture. Drizzle with olive oil and toss gently to coat evenly. Adjust seasoning with salt and pepper if necessary.

For enhanced flavors, cover the salad and refrigerate for about 30 minutes before serving.

Serving Suggestions:
This salad is a complete meal but can be served with whole-grain crackers for added crunch and fiber.

Consider pairing it with a cold herbal tea for a refreshing meal.

LUNCH

Roasted Tomato and Sardine Salad

 SERVES 4　 **PREP TIME** 20 MIN.　 **COOK TIME** 10 MIN.

Ingredients:
4 large tomatoes
2 tablespoons olive oil
2 cans of sardines in water
1 cup arugula
1 cup baby spinach
1/2 red onion
2 tablespoons balsamic vinegar
1 teaspoon Dijon mustard

Nutritional Information (Per Serving):

Calories: 240

Protein: 20 g

Carbohydrates: 27 g

Fats: 6 g

Fiber: 7 g

Cholesterol: 45 mg

Sodium: 300 mg

Potassium: 750 mg

Directions:
Heat one tablespoon of olive oil over medium heat in a large pot. Add the diced sweet potatoes and cook for about 5 minutes, stirring occasionally, until they soften.
Add the chopped onion, red bell pepper, and garlic to the pot. Cook for another 5 minutes until the onion is translucent.Increase the heat to medium-high and add the ground turkey. Cook, breaking it up with a spoon, until the turkey is browned and cooked through.
Stir in the black beans, diced tomatoes with their juice, tomato paste, chili powder, cumin, paprika, and cayenne pepper. Mix well to combine all the ingredients.
Pour in the chicken broth and bring the mixture to a boil. Reduce the heat to low and let simmer for about 30 minutes until the sweet potatoes are tender and the chili has thickened.

Serving Suggestions:
For a balanced meal, serve this chili with whole-grain bread or a small mixed-greens salad.

Turkey, Strawberry & Avocado Salad

 SERVES 4　 **PREP TIME** 15 MIN.　 **COOK TIME** 10 MIN.

Ingredients:
12 ounces cooked turkey breast
2 cups fresh strawberries
1 large avocado
4 cups mixed greens
1/4 cup slivered almonds
For the Dressing:
3 tablespoons balsamic vinegar
1 tablespoon olive oil

Nutritional Information (Per Serving):

Calories: 290

Protein: 23 g

Carbohydrates: 15 g

Fats: 16 g

Fiber: 5 g

Cholesterol: 55 mg

Sodium: 70 mg

Potassium: 650 mg

Directions:
Wash and dry the mixed greens thoroughly. Arrange them as a base in a large salad bowl or on individual plates.
Distribute the sliced turkey breast, strawberries, and diced avocado evenly over the greens.
In a small bowl, whisk together the balsamic vinegar, olive oil, and honey (if using) until well combined. Season lightly with salt and pepper if desired.
Drizzle the dressing over the salad. Toss gently to coat all ingredients, ensuring not to mash the avocado.Sprinkle the slivered almonds over the salad for added crunch and flavor (if using).

Serving Suggestions:
This salad is perfect for a light lunch or nutritious dinner.
Pair with a whole-grain roll or quinoa for a more filling meal.

LUNCH

Turkey Tabbouleh

 SERVES 4   **PREP TIME** 20 MIN.   **COOK TIME** 30 MIN.

Ingredients:
1 cup cooked bulgur wheat
12 ounces lean ground turkey
1 large cucumber, diced
2 large tomatoes, diced
1 bunch fresh parsley, finely c
hopped (about 1 cup)
1/4 cup fresh mint leaves, finely chopped
3 green onions, thinly sliced
Juice of 2 lemons
2 tablespoons olive oil

Nutritional Information
(Per Serving):

Calories: 320

Protein: 23 g

Carbohydrates: 30 g

Fats: 12 g

Fiber: 8 g

Cholesterol: 55 mg

Sodium: 75 mg

Potassium: 600 mg

Directions:
Prepare bulgur wheat according to package instructions.
Fluff with a fork and set aside to cool.
Over medium heat, cook the ground turkey in a non-stick
skillet until browned and cooked through, about 10 minutes.
Break it into small pieces as it cooks. Season with salt and
pepper if desired. Set aside to cool.
Combine the diced cucumber, tomatoes, chopped parsley,
mint, and green onions in a large bowl.
Add the cooled bulgur wheat and cooked turkey to the bowl
with the vegetables and herbs. Toss to combine.
Whisk the lemon juice, olive oil, and optional cayenne pepper
in a small bowl. Pour over the tabbouleh and mix well.
For best flavor, cover the tabbouleh and refrigerate for at
least 30 minutes before serving.

Serving Suggestions:
This turkey tabbouleh can be served as a complete meal,
perfect for lunch or a light dinner.
Pair with a yogurt or a slice of pita bread for a more filling
meal.

Healthy Lunch Wraps

 SERVES 4   **PREP TIME** 15 MIN.   **COOK TIME** 25 MIN.

Ingredients:
4 whole wheat tortillas (8-inch)
1 cup cooked chicken breast
1 large avocado, sliced
2 cups mixed salad greens
1 medium carrot
1/2 red bell pepper
1/4 cup red onion
1/4 cup fresh cilantro
2 tablespoons low-fat Greek yogurt
1 lime)
1/4 teaspoon cumin
Salt and pepper to taste

Nutritional Information
(Per Serving):

Calories: 280 kcal

Protein: 20 g

Carbohydrates: 34 g

Fat: 10 g

Fiber: 6 g

Cholesterol: 35 mg

Sodium: 220 mg

Potassium: 500 mg

Directions:
If not using precooked chicken, season chicken breast with
salt and pepper and lightly brush with olive oil. Grill over
medium heat for 5-6 minutes on each side until fully cooked
and juices run clear. Allow to cool slightly, and then shred
using two forks.
In a small bowl, combine Greek yogurt, lime juice, honey (if
using), and cumin. Stir until smooth. Adjust the seasoning
with salt and pepper to taste.
Lay out the whole wheat tortillas on a clean surface. Spread
each tortilla evenly with the yogurt lime dressing.Top with
an even layer of mixed greens, followed by shredded chicken, avocado slices, carrot, red bell pepper, red onion, and
cilantro.If using, sprinkle chia seeds and cucumber slices over
the filling.
Carefully fold in the sides of the tortilla and roll tightly to
enclose the filling. Cut each wrap in half diagonally.

Serving Suggestions:
Pair the wrap with fresh fruit or a small serving of unsalted
nuts for a balanced meal.

LUNCH

Sesame Soba Noodles

 SERVES 4   **PREP TIME** 10 MIN.   **COOK TIME** 20 MIN.

Ingredients:
8 oz soba noodles (buckwheat noodles)
2 cups shredded purple cabbage
1 large carrot, julienned
1 red bell pepper, thinly sliced
1/2 cup edamame, shelled and cooked
3 green onions
1/4 cup fresh cilantro
2 tablespoons toasted sesame seeds
3 tablespoons low-sodium soy sauce
2 tablespoons rice vinegar
1 tablespoon sesame oil
1 tablespoon ginger
1 garlic clove
1 tablespoon honey

Nutritional Information (Per Serving):
Calories: 320 kcal
Protein: 12 g
Carbohydrates: 48 g
Fat: 9 g
Fiber: 4 g
Cholesterol: 0 mg
Sodium: 300 mg
Potassium: 400 mg

Directions:
Bring a large pot of water to a boil. Add soba noodles and cook according to package instructions, usually 4-5 minutes. Drain and rinse under cold water to stop cooking and remove excess starch.

Whisk together soy sauce, rice vinegar, sesame oil, ginger, garlic, and honey in a small bowl. Add chili flakes if desired for extra heat.

Combine the cooked and cooled soba noodles, purple cabbage, carrot, red bell pepper, edamame, green onions, and cilantro in a large mixing bowl. Pour the sesame dressing over the noodle mixture and toss to coat evenly.

Sprinkle toasted sesame seeds (and crushed peanuts) over the noodles. For enhanced flavor, allow the noodles to chill in the refrigerator for about 30 minutes before serving to let the flavors meld.

Serve chilled or at room temperature. Garnish with lime zest if using for a refreshing citrus note.

Serving Suggestions:
This dish pairs well with a light soup, such as miso or a clear vegetable broth.

Fresh Spring Rolls

 SERVES 4   **PREP TIME** 20 MIN.   **COOK TIME** 30 MIN.

Ingredients:
8 rice paper wrappers
(8.5-inch diameter)
1 cup cooked shrimp
1 large carrot
1 cucumber
1 bell pepper
1 cup thinly sliced purple cabbage
1 avocado
1/4 cup fresh mint leaves
1/4 cup fresh basil leaves
1/4 cup fresh cilantro
3 tablespoons low-sodium soy sauce
2 tablespoons rice vinegar
1 tablespoon lime juice
1 garlic clove
1 teaspoon grated fresh ginger

Nutritional Information (Per Serving):
Calories: 200 kcal
Protein: 8 g
Carbohydrates: 28 g
Fat: 7 g (mostly from avocado, which provides healthy fats)
Fiber: 5 g
Cholesterol: 55 mg (from shrimp)
Sodium: 300 mg
Potassium: 400 mg

Directions:
Wash all vegetables and herbs. Julienne carrots, cucumber, and bell pepper. Slice cabbage thinly. Keep herbs whole or roughly chopped, depending on your preference.

In a small bowl, combine soy sauce, rice vinegar, lime juice, minced garlic, grated ginger, and honey. Add chili flakes for heat if desired. Set aside for flavors to meld.

Fill a large shallow dish with warm water. Dip one rice paper wrapper into the water for 15-20 seconds until it is pliable but not too soft.

Lay the softened wrapper on a clean, damp surface. Place a few pieces of shrimp on the lower third of the wrapper, followed by a small handful of carrots, cucumber, bell pepper, cabbage, and avocado. Add mint, basil, and cilantro leaves. Fold the bottom of the wrapper up over the filling, then fold in the sides and roll tightly. The wrapper will stick to itself. Repeat with remaining wrappers and filling.

Serving Suggestions:
Serve fresh spring rolls as a light and refreshing meal or appetizer. They pair well with additional vegetable sides or a clear soup for a fuller meal.

LUNCH

Best Buddha Bowl

 SERVES 4 **PREP TIME** 15 MIN. **COOK TIME** 30 MIN.

Ingredients:
1 cup quinoa
2 cups water
1 large sweet potato
1 tbsp olive oil
1 tsp smoked paprika
1/2 tsp garlic powder
Salt and pepper to taste
2 cups kale
1 tbsp lemon juice
1 cup canned chickpeas
1 medium beet
1 avocado
1/4 cup pumpkin seeds
1/4 cup tahini
2 tbsp water (or as needed for consistency)
1 tbsp apple cider vinegar
1 garlic clove

Nutritional Information (Per Serving):

Calories: 460 kcal

Protein: 15 g

Carbohydrates: 58 g

Fat: 20 g

Fiber: 12 g

Sodium: 300 mg

Potassium: 950 mg

Directions:
In a medium saucepan, bring 2 cups of water to a boil. Add the rinsed quinoa, reduce heat to low, cover, and simmer for about 15 minutes or until the water is absorbed. Remove from heat, let sit covered for 5 minutes, then fluff with a fork.
Preheat the oven to 400°F (200°C). Toss the cubed sweet potatoes with olive oil, smoked paprika, garlic powder, salt, and pepper. Spread on a baking sheet and roast for 25 minutes or until tender and slightly caramelized.
Massage the chopped kale with lemon juice and a pinch of salt in a large bowl until the leaves soften and wilt.
Spread the chickpeas on a baking sheet lined with parchment paper. Roast in the oven at 400°F for about 20 minutes or until crispy. In a small bowl, whisk together tahini, water, apple cider vinegar, honey (if using), and minced garlic until smooth. Adjust consistency with more water if needed.
Divide the cooked quinoa into four bowls. Arrange roasted sweet potatoes, massaged kale, crispy chickpeas, grated beet, and avocado slices in sections around the quinoa. Sprinkle it with toasted pumpkin seeds.Drizzle each bowl generously with tahini dressing. Add optional enhancements like chia seeds or a squeeze of fresh orange juice if desired.

Serving Suggestions:
This Buddha Bowl is a complete meal, offering a balanced mix of macronutrients and micronutrients. For a lighter version, you can reduce the portion sizes.

DINNER

Turkey Meatballs in Tomato Sauce

 SERVES 4   **PREP TIME** 20 MIN.   **COOK TIME** 40 MIN.

Ingredients:

1 pound (450g) lean ground turkey
1/2 cup oats, ground into flour
1 large egg white
1/4 cup fresh parsley
2 cloves garlic
1/2 cup onion
1 teaspoon dried oregano
1 teaspoon dried basil
1/4 teaspoon salt
1/4 teaspoon black pepper
1 tablespoon tomato paste
1 medium onion
2 cloves garlic
1 teaspoon dried oregano
1 teaspoon dried basil
1/2 teaspoon crushed red pepper flakes
1 tablespoon extra-virgin olive oil
1 cup water or low-sodium vegetable broth
1 can (28 ounces) no-salt-added crushed tomatoes

> **Nutritional Information (Per Serving):**
> Calories: 280
> Protein: 26g
> Carbohydrates: 23g
> Fats: 10g
> Fiber: 5g
> Cholesterol: 60mg
> Sodium: 290 mg
> Potassium: 700mg

Directions:

In a large bowl, mix the ground turkey, ground oats, egg white, parsley, minced garlic, chopped onion, oregano, basil, salt, and pepper.Form the mixture into 16 meatballs (about 1.5 inches in diameter). Place a non-stick skillet over medium heat and lightly coat with cooking spray. Brown the meatballs on all sides, about 5-7 minutes. They can be partially cooked through at this stage.In a separate larger pot, heat the olive oil over medium heat. Add the chopped onion and minced garlic, cooking until soft and translucent, about 3-4 minutes.Stir in the tomato paste and let it cook for 1 minute. Add the crushed tomatoes, oregano, basil, and red pepper flakes. Bring to a simmer and cook for 5 minutes.
Add the partially cooked meatballs to the sauce. Pour in water or broth to adjust the consistency as needed. Cover and let simmer gently for 25-30 minutes. Stir occasionally to prevent the sauce from sticking.

Serving Suggestions:

Serve the meatballs and sauce over a bed of cooked whole-grain pasta, zucchini noodles or alongside steamed

Spinach and Mushroom Stuffed Chicken

 SERVES 4   **PREP TIME** 25 MIN.   **COOK TIME** 30 MIN.

Ingredients:

4 boneless, skinless chicken breasts
2 cups fresh spinach
1 cup mushrooms
2 cloves garlic
1/4 cup onions
1/2 teaspoon dried thyme
1/2 teaspoon dried rosemary
1/4 teaspoon salt
1/4 teaspoon black pepper
1 tablespoon olive oil

> **Nutritional Information (Per Serving):**
> Calories: 230
> Protein: 29g
> Carbohydrates: 5g
> Fats: 9g (lower if feta is omitted)
> Fiber: 1.5g
> Cholesterol: 70mg
> Sodium: 280mg
> Potassium: 480mg

Directions:

Preheat your oven to 375°F (190°C).In a large skillet, heat the olive oil over medium heat. Add the onions and garlic and sauté until they soften, about 2-3 minutes.Add the chopped mushrooms and cook until they are soft, about 5 minutes.Stir in the spinach, thyme, and rosemary. Cook until the spinach has wilted, about 2 minutes. Remove from heat and let the mixture cool slightly. If using, stir in the low-fat feta cheese. Butterfly each chicken breast: cut horizontally, stopping just before you cut through so you can open them like a book. Place each breast between two pieces of plastic wrap and gently pound with a flat side of a meat mallet or rolling pin until about 1/4 inch thick.
Divide the spinach and mushroom mixture evenly among the chicken breasts, spreading it over one-half of each opened breast.Fold the other half over the stuffing and secure with toothpicks.
Place the stuffed breasts in a bakings dish sprayed with non-stick cooking spray.Season the outside of the chicken with salt and pepper.Bake in the preheated oven until the chicken is cooked and reaches an internal temperature of 165°F (75°C), about 25-30 minutes.

Serving Suggestions:

For a complete meal, serve the stuffed chicken with steamed green beans or a fresh green salad.

DINNER

Ginger and Garlic Grilled Salmon

 SERVES 4   **PREP TIME** 15 MIN.   **COOK TIME** 10 MIN.

Ingredients:
4 salmon filets, skin-on
2 tablespoons fresh ginger
3 cloves garlic
2 tablespoons low-sodium soy sauce
1 tablespoon olive oil
1 tablespoon lemon juice
1/2 teaspoon black pepper

Nutritional Information (Per Serving):

Calories: 280

Protein: 23g

Carbohydrates: 4g

Fats: 18g

Fiber: 0.5g

Cholesterol: 55mg

Sodium: 320mg

Potassium: 500mg

Directions:
Combine the grated ginger, minced garlic, low-sodium soy sauce, olive oil, lemon juice, black pepper, and optional honey or maple syrup in a small bowl. Mix well.Place the salmon filets in a shallow dish or a resealable plastic bag. Pour the marinade over the salmon, ensuring all surfaces are coated.Refrigerate and let marinate for at least 30 minutes or 2 hours for more flavor.
Preheat an outdoor grill or a grill pan over medium-high heat. If using an outdoor grill, lightly oil the grate to prevent sticking.
Remove the salmon from the marinade, letting excess drip off. Place skin-side down on the grill.Grill for 4-5 minutes per side or until the salmon is fully cooked and flakes quickly with a fork. The exact cooking time may vary depending on the thickness of the filets.

Serving Suggestions:
Serve the grilled salmon with a side of mixed greens dressed with a light vinaigrette and a serving of quinoa or steamed vegetables like asparagus or broccoli

Salmon En Papillote with Potatoes

 SERVES 4   **PREP TIME** 20 MIN.   **COOK TIME** 30 MIN.

Ingredients:
4 salmon filets, skinless
4 small potatoes
1 large carrot
1 zucchini
1 red bell pepper
2 tablespoons olive oil
4 teaspoons fresh lemon juice
4 cloves garlic
2 tablespoons fresh dill
Salt and pepper to taste

Nutritional Information (Per Serving):

Calories: 350

Protein: 24g

Carbohydrates: 28g

Fats: 15g

Fiber: 4g

Cholesterol: 55mg

Sodium: 150mg

Potassium: 900mg

Directions:
Preheat your oven to 400°F (200°C).
Thinly slice the potatoes, carrots, zucchini, and red bell pepper. This ensures they cook quickly and evenly.
Cut four large pieces of parchment paper or aluminum foil, each large enough to fold over and seal the salmon and vegetables.Layer the vegetables on each piece, starting with potatoes and then carrots, zucchini, and bell pepper.Top each vegetable pile with a salmon filet. Drizzle each filet with one teaspoon of lemon juice and 1/2 tablespoon of olive oil—season with salt, pepper, and minced garlic.Sprinkle chopped dill (and optional parsley or thyme) over the top.
Fold the parchment paper or foil over the salmon and vegetables, pinching the edges to seal the packets completely. This keeps the steam inside for moist cooking.
Place the packets on a baking sheet and bake in the preheated oven for about 20-25 minutes, until the salmon is cooked and the vegetables are tender.

Serving Suggestions:
Carefully open the packets (watch for steam), and serve immediately.
Ideal with a side of mixed greens or a light cucumber salad for added freshness and fiber.

DINNER

Garlicky Lemon Oven Baked Tilapia

 SERVES 4   **PREP TIME** 10 MIN.   **COOK TIME** 15 MIN.

Ingredients:
4 tilapia filets
4 cloves garlic
2 tablespoons fresh lemon juice
1 tablespoon olive oil
1/4 teaspoon black pepper
1/2 teaspoon paprika
1/4 cup fresh parsley

Nutritional Information (Per Serving):

Calories: 200

Protein: 23g

Carbohydrates: 2g

Fats: 10g

Fiber: 0.5g

Cholesterol: 55mg

Sodium: 60mg

Potassium: 380mg

Directions:
Preheat your oven to 400°F (200°C).
Rinse the tilapia filets and pat dry with paper towels. This ensures proper seasoning adherence and even cooking.
Combine the minced garlic, lemon juice, olive oil, black pepper, and paprika in a small bowl. Mix well to create the marinade.Place the tilapia filets in a baking dish in a single layer. Brush each filet generously with the marinade, ensuring all surfaces are well coated.
Bake in the oven for 12-15 minutes or until the fish flakes easily with a fork. The exact time may depend on the thickness of the filets.

Serving Suggestions:
Sprinkle the baked tilapia with chopped fresh parsley. Add lemon slices on top or alongside for extra zest if desired.
Serve hot with steamed vegetables like broccoli or green beans and perhaps a portion of whole-grain couscous or a fresh salad for a complete meal.

Shrimp Bowls with Brown Rice

 SERVES 4   **PREP TIME** 20 MIN.   **COOK TIME** 45 MIN.

Ingredients:
1 cup brown rice
1 pound shrimp
2 tablespoons olive oil
2 cloves garlic
1 medium onion
1 red bell pepper
1 cup broccoli florets
1 carrot
2 teaspoons soy sauce, low sodium
1 teaspoon sesame oil
1/2 teaspoon ground ginger

Nutritional Information (Per Serving):

Calories: 350

Protein: 24g

Carbohydrates: 45g

Fats: 8g

Fiber: 4g

Cholesterol: 180mg

Sodium: 300mg

Potassium: 400mg

Directions:
Rinse the brown rice under cold water until the water runs clear.Bring 2 1/4 cups of water to a boil in a medium pot. Add the rinsed rice, reduce heat to low, cover, and simmer for about 40-45 minutes, or until the water is absorbed and the rice is tender.
While the rice cooks, heat one tablespoon of olive oil in a large skillet over medium heat.Add the minced garlic and chopped onion, sautéing until the onion becomes translucent, about 3-4 minutes.Increase the heat to medium-high and add the shrimp. Cook until they are pink and opaque, about 2-3 minutes per side. Remove the shrimp and set aside.
In the same skillet, add another tablespoon of olive oil. Toss in the red bell pepper, broccoli, and carrot. Stir-fry for about 5-7 minutes until the vegetables are tender-crisp.Return the shrimp to the skillet. Add soy sauce, sesame oil, and ground ginger. Stir well to combine and heat through, about two more minutes.

Serving Suggestions:
Serve hot, with a side of mixed greens or a small fresh salad to add more fiber and nutrients.

DINNER

Broiled Tilapia with Thai Coconut Curry Sauce

 SERVES 4   **PREP TIME** 15 MIN.   **COOK TIME** 15 MIN.

Ingredients:
4 tilapia filets
1 tablespoon olive oil
Salt and pepper to taste
1 cup light coconut milk
1 tablespoon red curry paste
1 teaspoon fresh ginger
2 cloves garlic
1 tablespoon low-sodium soy sauce
1 teaspoon lime juice
1/2 teaspoon honey
1/4 cup chopped fresh cilantro

Nutritional Information (Per Serving):

Calories: 280

Protein: 23g

Carbohydrates: 8g

Fats: 15g

Fiber: 1g

Cholesterol: 55mg

Sodium: 250mg

Potassium: 500mg

Directions:
Set your oven's broiler high and let it preheat while preparing the fish and sauce.

Pat the tilapia filets dry with paper towels and place them on a lightly greased broiling pan.Brush each filet with olive oil and season lightly with salt and pepper.Broil in the preheated oven for 6-7 minutes or until the fish flakes easily with a fork. There is no need to turn the filets.

While the fish is broiling, heat a small saucepan over medium heat.Add the red curry paste, grated ginger, and minced garlic to the pan. Sauté for about 1 minute until fragrant.

Stir in the light coconut milk, low-sodium soy sauce, and lime juice. Bring to a gentle simmer, not a boil, and let it cook for about 5 minutes to combine the flavors.If using honey, stir it in at the end of cooking.

Once the tilapia is cooked, remove from the oven.Spoon the warm Thai coconut curry sauce over the broiled tilapia filets.

Serving Suggestions:
Serve with steamed jasmine rice or cauliflower rice for those controlling carbohydrate intake more strictly.

A side of steamed vegetables such as broccoli or spinach can complement this dish to increase fiber intake.

Simple Tilapia Skillet

 SERVES 4   **PREP TIME** 10 MIN.   **COOK TIME** 20 MIN.

Ingredients:
4 tilapia filets
1 tablespoon olive oil
2 cloves garlic
1 red bell pepper
1 medium zucchini
1 cup cherry tomatoes
1 lemon, zested and juiced
1/4 cup fresh parsley

Nutritional Information (Per Serving):

Calories: 220 kcal

Protein: 34 g

Carbohydrates: 8 g

Fats: 6 g

Fiber: 2 g

Cholesterol: 85 mg

Sodium: 125 mg

Potassium: 840 mg

Directions:
Wash and slice the red bell pepper and zucchini. Halve the cherry tomatoes and mince the garlic.

Pat the tilapia filets dry with paper towels—season both sides with salt and pepper.

Heat olive oil over medium heat in a large skillet. Add garlic and cook for about 1 minute until fragrant. Add the bell pepper and zucchini, sautéing for about 5 minutes until they soften.

Push the vegetables to the side of the skillet. Place the tilapia filets in the center and cook for about 3 minutes per side or until the fish flakes easily with a fork.

Add the cherry tomatoes and sprinkle the red pepper flakes (if using) over the skillet. Cook for an additional 3 minutes until the tomatoes are just soft.

Remove from heat. Drizzle lemon juice over the tilapia and vegetables and sprinkle with lemon zest and fresh parsley.

Serving Suggestions:
Serve this dish with a side of quinoa or a mixed green salad dressed lightly with vinaigrette to maintain a balanced meal that is low in fat and fiber.

DINNER

Rolled Turkey Breasts with Herby Lemon & Pine Nut Stuffing

 SERVES 6   **PREP TIME** 30 MIN.   **COOK TIME** 1 HOUR 15 MIN.

Ingredients:
2 lbs turkey breast, skinless
1 tablespoon olive oil
1/2 cup pine nuts
1 onion
2 cloves garlic
1 cup whole grain breadcrumbs
Zest of 1 lemon
Juice of 1/2 lemon
1/4 cup fresh parsley
1 tablespoon fresh thyme
1 tablespoon fresh rosemary

Nutritional Information (Per Serving):

Calories: 290 kcal

Protein: 35 g

Carbohydrates: 14 g

Fats: 12 g

Fiber: 3 g

Cholesterol: 70 mg

Sodium: 200 mg

Potassium: 450 mg

Directions:
Heat a skillet over medium heat. Add pine nuts and toast them until golden, about 3 minutes, then set aside. In the same skillet, add olive oil, onion, and garlic. Sauté until the onion is translucent, about 5 minutes. Combine toasted pine nuts, sautéed onion and garlic, breadcrumbs, lemon zest, lemon juice, parsley, thyme, rosemary, salt, and pepper in a bowl. Mix until well combined.

Lay the turkey breast flat on a cutting board. If it is too thick, butterfly the meat by slicing it horizontally but not all the way through, and open it like a book. Place plastic wrap over the turkey and gently pound it with a meat mallet to an even thickness of about 1/2 inch.

Spread the stuffing evenly over the turkey, leaving a small border around the edges. Roll the turkey over the stuffing, starting from one end to the other, and secure with kitchen twine or skewers.

Preheat the oven to 375°F (190°C). Place the rolled turkey in a roasting pan, brush with olive oil, and season with additional salt and pepper. Roast in the preheated oven for about 1 hour to 1 hour and 15 minutes, or until the internal temperature reaches 165°F (74°C).

Let the turkey rest for 10 minutes before slicing. Cut into 1-inch thick slices and serve.

Serving Suggestions:
Serve the turkey with a side of steamed vegetables, such as green beans or carrots, and a portion of wild rice or a fresh salad.

Honey Garlic Chicken Thighs with Carrots and Broccoli

 SERVES 4   **PREP TIME** 15 MIN.   **COOK TIME** 40 MIN.

Ingredients:
4 boneless, skinless chicken thighs
1 tablespoon olive oil
2 tablespoons honey
3 cloves garlic
1 tablespoon apple cider vinegar
1 tablespoon low-sodium soy sauce
1 tablespoon fresh ginger
1/2 teaspoon black pepper
2 cups carrots
2 cups broccoli florets

Nutritional Information (Per Serving):

Calories: 320 kcal

Protein: 28 g

Carbohydrates: 20 g

Fats: 12 g

Fiber: 3 g

Cholesterol: 140 mg

Sodium: 240 mg

Potassium: 550 mg

Directions:
Combine honey, minced garlic, apple cider vinegar, low-sodium soy sauce, grated ginger, and black pepper in a bowl. Mix well. Add the chicken thighs to the marinade and coat them well. Let them marinate for at least 30 minutes in the refrigerator.

Wash and slice the carrots. Cut the broccoli into florets.

Heat olive oil in a large skillet over medium heat. Remove the chicken from the marinade (keep the marinade) and sear the thighs for about 5 minutes on each side until golden brown.

Add the remaining marinade to the skillet along with the carrots. Cover and let simmer for 10 minutes. Add the broccoli, cover, and cook for another 10 minutes, until the vegetables are tender and the chicken is cooked.

Serving Suggestions:
Serve this dish with brown rice or quinoa to maintain a meal rich in fiber and whole grains.

DINNER

Chicken Florentine Style

 SERVES 4   **PREP TIME** 15 MIN.   **COOK TIME** 25 MIN.

Ingredients:
4 boneless, skinless chicken breasts
1 tablespoon olive oil
4 cloves garlic
3 cups fresh spinach
1 cup low-sodium chicken broth
1/2 cup fat-free Greek yogurt
1 tablespoon all-purpose flour
1 tablespoon lemon juice
1/2 teaspoon grated nutmeg

Nutritional Information (Per Serving):

Calories: 250 kcal

Protein: 29 g

Carbohydrates: 8 g

Fats: 10 g

Fiber: 2 g

Cholesterol: 75 mg

Sodium: 220 mg

Potassium: 500 mg

Directions:
Season the chicken breasts with salt and pepper. Heat olive oil in a large skillet over medium-high heat. Add the chicken and cook until golden and no longer pink in the center, about 5-7 minutes per side. Remove the chicken from the skillet and set aside.

In the same skillet, reduce heat to medium. Add minced garlic and cook until fragrant, about 1 minute. Add the fresh spinach and sauté until wilted, about 2-3 minutes.

Whisk together the Greek yogurt, flour, lemon juice, and nutmeg in a small bowl until smooth. Pour the low-sodium chicken broth into the skillet and bring to a simmer. Gradually add the yogurt mixture to the skillet, stirring constantly. Cook for 5 minutes until the sauce thickens.

Return the chicken to the skillet. Spoon the sauce and spinach over the chicken. Cover and simmer for another 5 minutes to ensure the chicken is thoroughly cooked and the flavors meld.

Serving Suggestions:
Pair this dish with a side of whole grain pasta or wild rice. Alternatively, a fresh garden salad can complement the dish's creamy texture.

Chicken Fried Rice

 SERVES 4   **PREP TIME** 15 MIN.   **COOK TIME** 20 MIN.

Ingredients:
2 cups cooked brown rice
2 boneless, skinless chicken breasts
1 tablespoon olive oil
1 large onion
2 cloves garlic
1 cup carrots
1 cup peas
2 eggs
2 tablespoons low-sodium soy sauce
1 tablespoon sesame oil
1/2 teaspoon black pepper

Nutritional Information (Per Serving):

Calories: 350 kcal

Protein: 27 g

Carbohydrates: 38 g

Fats: 11 g

Fiber: 5 g

Cholesterol: 120 mg

Sodium: 320 mg

Potassium: 500 mg

Directions:
Cook brown rice according to package instructions, preferably the day before, and refrigerate overnight to improve texture and reduce stickiness.

Heat olive oil in a large skillet or wok over medium-high heat. Add diced chicken and cook until browned and cooked through about 5-7 minutes. Remove chicken from the skillet and set aside.

In the same skillet, add more olive oil if needed. Sauté onions and garlic until translucent, about 2 minutes. Add diced carrots and cook for another 3-4 minutes until they soften. Stir in peas and cooked chicken, heating through. Push the vegetables to the side of the skillet. Pour the beaten eggs into the center and scramble until just set. Add the chilled brown rice, breaking up clumps. Stir everything together.

Drizzle the low-sodium soy sauce and sesame oil over the rice mixture. Season with black pepper and stir until everything is well mixed and heated through. If using, sprinkle chopped green onions on top for garnish.

Serving Suggestions:
Serve hot as a main dish. For added fiber and nutrients, accompany with a side of steamed broccoli or a fresh cucumber salad.

DINNER

Feta, Spinach & Tomato Stuffed Salmon Recipe

 SERVES 4　　 **PREP TIME** 15 MIN.　　 **COOK TIME** 20 MIN.

Ingredients:
4 salmon filets
2 cups fresh spinach
1/2 cup cherry tomatoes
1/4 cup feta cheese (low-fat)
1 tablespoon olive oil
2 cloves garlic
1 teaspoon dried oregano

Nutritional Information (Per Serving):

Calories: 320 kcal

Protein: 27 g

Carbohydrates: 4 g

Fats: 22 g

Fiber: 1 g

Cholesterol: 80 mg

Sodium: 200 mg

Potassium: 600 mg

Directions:
Preheat your oven to 375°F (190°C).
Heat olive oil in a skillet over medium heat. Add minced garlic and sauté until fragrant, about 1 minute.Add the chopped spinach and cook until wilted, about 2-3 minutes. Remove from heat.Stir in the diced cherry tomatoes, crumbled feta cheese, and oregano. Season with salt and pepper to taste.
Slice a pocket into the side of each salmon filet, being careful not to cut all the way through.Stuff each pocket generously with the spinach, tomato, and feta mixture.
Place the stuffed salmon filets on a baking sheet lined with parchment paper.Bake in the oven for 15-20 minutes or until the salmon is cooked and flakes easily with a fork.

Serving Suggestions:
Accompany the stuffed salmon with a side of quinoa or a mixed green salad dressed with a light vinaigrette.

Slow Cooker Salmon with Vegetables Recipe

SERVES 4　　**PREP TIME** 10 MIN.　　**COOK TIME** 2 hours on high or 4 hours on low

Ingredients:
4 salmon filets
2 lemons
2 cloves garlic
1 fennel bulb
2 cups cherry tomatoes
1 cup low-sodium vegetable broth
2 tablespoons fresh dill
Salt and pepper, to taste

Nutritional Information (Per Serving):

Calories: 280 kcal

Protein: 23 g

Carbohydrates: 8 g

Fats: 16 g

Fiber: 3 g

Cholesterol: 60 mg

Sodium: 180 mg

Potassium: 800 mg

Directions:
Rinse the salmon filets and pat dry. Season both sides with salt and pepper.Thinly slice the lemons and fennel bulb. Mince the garlic.
Place half of the lemon slices at the bottom of the slow cooker.Add the sliced fennel and minced garlic over the lemons. Place the salmon filets on top of the fennel. Arrange the remaining lemon slices and cherry tomatoes around and on top of the salmon.
Pour the low-sodium vegetable broth over the ingredients in the slow cooker.Sprinkle the chopped dill over everything. Cover and cook on high for 2 hours or on low for 4 hours. The salmon should be cooked through and flake easily with a fork.

Serving Suggestions:
For a complete meal, serve the salmon with a side of steamed asparagus or green beans and a portion of whole-grain couscous or quinoa.

DINNER

Baked Chilean Sea Bass

 SERVES 4　 **PREP TIME** 15 MIN.　 **COOK TIME** 20 MIN.

Ingredients:
4 Chilean sea bass filets
1 tablespoon olive oil
2 cloves garlic
1 lemon
1/2 cup fresh parsley
2 tablespoons capers
Salt and pepper, to taste
2 cups cherry tomatoes
1 cup asparagus, trimmed and
cut into 1-inch pieces

**Nutritional Information
(Per Serving):**

Calories: 290 kcal

Protein: 23 g

Carbohydrates: 6 g

Fats: 20 g

Fiber: 2 g

Cholesterol: 70 mg

Sodium: 200 mg

Potassium: 600 mg

Directions:
Preheat your oven to 400°F (200°C).
In a small bowl, mix the olive oil, minced garlic, half of the lemon juice, lemon zest, parsley, capers, and red pepper flakes (if using)—season with salt and pepper to taste.
Toss the cherry tomatoes and asparagus pieces in a separate bowl with a bit of olive oil and salt.
Lay the sea bass filets in a baking dish. Spoon the garlic and herb mixture over the filets.Scatter the seasoned tomatoes and asparagus around the fish.
Place the baking dish in the oven and bake for about 15-20 minutes, or until the fish is opaque and flakes easily with a fork.

Serving Suggestions:
Serve this dish with a side of quinoa or a mixed greens salad to maintain a balanced meal that supports liver health.

Cilantro-Lime Shrimp Tacos Recipe

 SERVES 4　 **PREP TIME** 15 MIN.　 **COOK TIME** 10 MIN.

Ingredients:
1 pound shrimp
1 tablespoon olive oil
Juice of 2 limes
1/4 cup fresh cilantro
2 cloves garlic
1 teaspoon chili powder
1/2 teaspoon ground cumin
Salt and pepper, to taste
8 small whole wheat tortillas
1 avocado
1 cup cabbage
1/2 cup cherry tomatoes

**Nutritional Information
(Per Serving):**

Calories: 350 kcal

Protein: 25 g

Carbohydrates: 35 g

Fats: 12 g

Fiber: 7 g

Cholesterol: 180 mg

Sodium: 300 mg

Potassium: 400 mg

Directions:
Combine shrimp, olive oil, half the lime juice, cilantro, garlic, chili powder, cumin, salt, and pepper in a bowl. Mix well to coat the shrimp. Let it marinate for at least 10 minutes.
Slice the avocado, shred the cabbage, and halve the cherry tomatoes. Set aside.
Heat a large skillet over medium-high heat. Add the marinated shrimp and cook for 2-3 minutes on each side or until the shrimp are pink and cooked through.
Warm the whole wheat tortillas in the oven or on a skillet for a few seconds on each side.Divide the cooked shrimp among the tortillas.Top each taco with avocado slices, shredded cabbage, and cherry tomatoes.Drizzle with the remaining lime juice and add a dollop of Greek yogurt.

Serving Suggestions:
Serve these tacos with black beans or a fresh corn salad for a fiber-rich, balanced meal.

DINNER

Chargrilled Mackerel with Sweet & Sour Beetroot

 SERVES 4   **PREP TIME** 20 MIN.   **COOK TIME** 15 MIN.

Ingredients:
4 fresh mackerel filets
1 tablespoon olive oil
Salt and pepper, to taste
2 cups fresh beetroot
1 red onion
1/4 cup apple cider vinegar
2 tablespoons honey
1 teaspoon mustard seeds
1 orange, zest and juice

Nutritional Information (Per Serving):

Calories: 350 kcal

Protein: 23 g

Carbohydrates: 18 g

Fats: 20 g

Fiber: 3 g

Cholesterol: 85 mg

Sodium: 200 mg

Potassium: 650 mg

Directions:
Combine grated beetroot, red onion, apple cider vinegar, honey, mustard seeds, and half of the orange juice and zest in a saucepan.Cook over medium heat for 10-15 minutes, stirring occasionally, until the beetroot is tender and the liquid has reduced to a syrupy consistency.
Preheat a grill or grill pan over high heat.
Brush the mackerel filets with olive oil and season with salt and pepper.
Place the mackerel filets skin side down on the grill. Grill for 3-4 minutes on each side or until the skin is crisp and the flesh is cooked.
Divide the sweet and sour beetroot among plates.Top with the grilled mackerel filets.Garnish with the remaining orange zest and optional fresh dill or parsley.Drizzle any remaining orange juice over the top.

Serving Suggestions:
Serve with a side of steamed green beans or a fresh green salad for a balanced meal.

Mackerel with Warm Cauliflower & Caper Salad

 SERVES 4   **PREP TIME** 15 MIN. **COOK TIME** 25 MIN.

Ingredients:
4 fresh mackerel filets
1 large head of cauliflower
2 tablespoons olive oil
1/4 cup capers
2 tablespoons red wine vinegar
1 teaspoon Dijon mustard
1 small red onion
1/4 cup chopped fresh parsley
Salt and pepper, to taste

Nutritional Information (Per Serving):

Calories: 350 kcal

Protein: 24 g

Carbohydrates: 12 g

Fats: 22 g

Fiber: 5 g

Cholesterol: 80 mg

Sodium: 300 mg

Potassium: 750 mg

Directions:
Preheat the oven to 425°F (220°C).Toss the cauliflower florets with one tablespoon of olive oil, salt, and pepper.Spread the cauliflower on a baking sheet in a single layer and roast for about 20 minutes until tender and slightly golden.
Whisk together the remaining olive oil, red wine vinegar, Dijon mustard, and a pinch of salt and pepper in a small bowl. Set aside.
While the cauliflower is roasting, heat a non-stick skillet over medium-high heat.Season the mackerel filets with salt and pepper.Place the mackerel skin-side down in the skillet. Cook for about 3-4 minutes per side or until the skin is crispy and the fish is cooked through.
Combine the roasted cauliflower, sliced red onion, capers, and chopped parsley in a large bowl.Drizzle the dressing over the salad and toss gently to combine.

Serving Suggestions:
A side of mixed greens or steamed green beans complement this dish well, enhancing its nutritional value without adding significant calories.

DINNER

Chicken & Broccoli Quinoa Casserole

 SERVES 6   **PREP TIME** 20 MIN.   **COOK TIME** 30 MIN.

Ingredients:
1 cup quinoa
2 cups low-sodium chicken broth
1 tablespoon olive oil
1 medium onion
2 cloves garlic
2 cups broccoli florets
2 cups cooked chicken breast
1 cup low-fat Greek yogurt
1/2 cup milk (skim or 1%)
1 teaspoon dried thyme
1/2 teaspoon paprika
Salt and pepper, to taste

Nutritional Information (Per Serving):

Calories: 290 kcal

Protein: 27 g

Carbohydrates: 25 g

Fats: 9 g

Fiber: 4 g

Cholesterol: 55 mg

Sodium: 220 mg

Potassium: 500 mg

Directions:
In a saucepan, bring the chicken broth to a boil. Add the quinoa, reduce heat to low, cover, and simmer for 15 minutes or until the liquid is absorbed and the quinoa is tender. Preheat your oven to 375°F (190°C).
While the quinoa is cooking, heat olive oil in a skillet over medium heat. Add the onion and garlic, and sauté until the onion is translucent, about 5 minutes. Add the broccoli and cook for an additional 5 minutes until slightly tender.
Combine the cooked quinoa, sautéed vegetables, diced chicken, Greek yogurt, milk, thyme, paprika, salt, and pepper in a large bowl. Mix well to ensure everything is evenly distributed.
Transfer the mixture to a greased baking dish. If using, sprinkle the top with grated Parmesan cheese.
Bake in the preheated oven for 30 minutes or until the top is

Serving Suggestions:
Serve this casserole with a side salad of mixed greens dressed with a light vinaigrette to add freshness and fiber.

Baked Chicken with Brussels Sprouts

 SERVES 4   **PREP TIME** 10 MIN.   **COOK TIME** 40 MIN.

Ingredients:
4 boneless, skinless chicken breasts
1 tablespoon olive oil
1 pound Brussels sprouts
1 lemon
4 cloves garlic
1 teaspoon dried thyme
Salt and pepper, to taste

Nutritional Information (Per Serving):

Calories: 280 kcal

Protein: 26 g

Carbohydrates: 12 g

Fats: 12 g

Fiber: 4 g

Cholesterol: 75 mg

Sodium: 300 mg

Potassium: 700 mg

Directions:
Preheat your oven to 400°F (200°C).
Pat the chicken breasts dry with paper towels. Season both sides with salt, pepper, and dried thyme.
Toss the Brussels sprouts with olive oil, minced garlic, salt, and pepper in a large bowl.
Arrange the seasoned Brussels sprouts in a single layer on a large baking sheet. Place the seasoned chicken breasts among the Brussels sprouts. Distribute lemon slices around the chicken and Brussels sprouts for added flavor.
Bake in the preheated oven for about 35-40 minutes, or until the chicken is thoroughly cooked (reaching an internal temperature of 165°F or 74°C) and Brussels sprouts are tender and caramelized.

Serving Suggestions:
For a complete meal, serve this dish with a side of quinoa or brown rice, or for a lower carbohydrate option, a mixed green salad with a light vinaigrette.

DINNER

Golden Cauliflower Chicken Curry

 SERVES 4   **PREP TIME** 15 MIN.   **COOK TIME** 30 MIN.

Ingredients:
1 tablespoon olive oil
1 large onion
3 cloves garlic
1 tablespoon fresh ginger
1 tablespoon turmeric
1 teaspoon ground cumin
1/2 teaspoon ground coriander
1/4 teaspoon cayenne pepper
1 pound chicken breast
1 large head of cauliflower
1 can (14 ounces) of light coconut milk
1 cup low-sodium chicken broth
Salt and pepper, to taste
1/2 cup frozen peas
2 tablespoons fresh cilantro
Juice of 1 lime

Nutritional Information (Per Serving):
Calories: 290 kcal
Protein: 27 g
Carbohydrates: 18 g
Fats: 12 g
Fiber: 6 g
Cholesterol: 60 mg
Sodium: 200 mg
Potassium: 800 mg

Directions:
Heat the olive oil in a large skillet over medium heat. Add the onion and cook until translucent, about 5 minutes. Add the garlic and ginger, cooking for another minute until fragrant.
Stir in the turmeric, cumin, coriander, and cayenne pepper. Cook for about 1 minute until the spices are well combined and aromatic.
Add the chicken pieces to the skillet, seasoning with salt and pepper. Cook until the chicken is browned on all sides, about 5-7 minutes.
Add the cauliflower florets to the skillet, coconut milk and chicken broth. Bring the mixture to a simmer, then reduce the heat and cover. Let it simmer gently for about 20 minutes or until the cauliflower is tender.
Stir in the frozen peas and cook for an additional 5 minutes. Remove from heat and stir in the fresh cilantro and lime juice.

Serving Suggestions:
Serve this curry over a bed of steamed brown rice or cauliflower rice for a low-carb option. Add a side of mango chutney for a sweetness without significant fat.

Balsamic Glazed Chicken and Roasted Vegetables

 SERVES 4   **PREP TIME** 15 MIN.   **COOK TIME** 30 MIN.

Ingredients:
4 boneless, skinless chicken breasts
1 tablespoon olive oil
1/4 cup balsamic vinegar
2 tablespoons honey
2 cloves garlic
1 teaspoon dried rosemary
Salt and pepper, to taste
2 cups Brussels sprouts
2 medium carrots
1 red bell pepper
1 zucchini, cut into half-moons

Nutritional Information (Per Serving):
Calories: 320 kcal
Protein: 27 g
Carbohydrates: 25 g
Fats: 9 g
Fiber: 5 g
Cholesterol: 65 mg
Sodium: 200 mg
Potassium: 800 mg

Directions:
Preheat your oven to 425°F (220°C).
Mix the balsamic vinegar, honey, minced garlic, and dried rosemary in a small bowl—season with salt and pepper.
Rub each chicken breast with olive oil, then season with salt and pepper. Could you place them in a large baking dish? Toss the Brussels sprouts, carrots, red bell pepper, and zucchini in olive oil and season with salt and pepper. Scatter the vegetables around the chicken in the baking dish.
Brush the balsamic glaze generously over the chicken breasts. Place the dish in the preheated oven and roast for about 25-30 minutes, or until the chicken is cooked through (internal temperature of 165°F or 74°C) and the vegetables are tender and caramelized.

Serving Suggestions:
This dish pairs well with a side of quinoa or brown rice, which absorbs the delicious balsamic glaze and provides a hearty, fiber-rich meal.

DINNER

Easy Honey Garlic Chicken Stir-Fry

 SERVES 4   **PREP TIME** 10 MIN.   **COOK TIME** 15 MIN.

Ingredients:
2 tablespoons olive oil
1 pound boneless, skinless chicken breasts
Salt and pepper, to taste
3 cloves garlic
1 tablespoon fresh ginger
1/4 cup low-sodium soy sauce
2 tablespoons honey
1 tablespoon apple cider vinegar
1 cup broccoli florets
1 red bell pepper
1 carrot
1/2 cup snow peas
1 teaspoon sesame seeds
2 green onions

Nutritional Information (Per Serving):
Calories: 280 kcal
Protein: 27 g
Carbohydrates: 18 g
Fats: 10 g
Fiber: 3 g
Cholesterol: 65 mg
Sodium: 300 mg
Potassium: 500 mg

Directions:
Mix the soy sauce, honey, and apple cider vinegar in a small bowl. Set aside.
Heat 1 tablespoon of olive oil in a large skillet or wok over medium-high heat. Season the chicken slices with salt and pepper. Add to the skillet and stir-fry until the chicken is browned and cooked through about 5-7 minutes. Remove the chicken from the skillet and set aside.
In the same skillet, add the remaining tablespoon of olive oil. Add the garlic and ginger, and stir-fry for about 30 seconds or until fragrant. Add the broccoli, bell pepper, carrot, and snow peas. Stir-fry for about 5 minutes or until the vegetables are just tender.
Return the chicken to the skillet. Pour the prepared sauce over the chicken and vegetables. Stir well to combine and cook for another 2-3 minutes, until everything is heated and the sauce has thickened slightly.
Sprinkle with sesame seeds and sliced green onions if using.

Serving Suggestions:
Serve this stir-fry over a bed of steamed brown rice or cauliflower rice for a lower-carbohydrate option.

Healthy Apricot Chicken

 SERVES 4   **PREP TIME** 10 MIN.   **COOK TIME** 25 MIN.

Ingredients:
4 boneless, skinless chicken breasts
1 tablespoon olive oil
Salt and pepper, to taste
1 onion
2 cloves garlic
1 cup fresh apricots, diced
 (or 3/4 cup dried apricots, soaked and chopped)
1/2 cup low-sodium chicken broth
2 tablespoons apple cider vinegar
1 tablespoon fresh rosemary
1 teaspoon Dijon mustard

Nutritional Information (Per Serving):
Calories: 260 kcal
Protein: 26 g
Carbohydrates: 18 g
Fats: 8 g
Fiber: 3 g
Cholesterol: 65 mg
Sodium: 200 mg
Potassium: 500 mg

Directions:
Season the chicken breasts with salt and pepper.
Heat the olive oil in a large skillet over medium heat. Add the chicken breasts and cook until golden on both sides, about 3-4 minutes per side. Remove the chicken and set aside.
In the same skillet, add the chopped onion and minced garlic. Cook until the onion is translucent, about 5 minutes. Add the diced apricots to the skillet with the onions and garlic. Stir in the chicken broth, apple cider vinegar, rosemary, Dijon mustard, and optional red pepper flakes. Bring to a simmer.
Return the chicken to the skillet, spooning the sauce over the breasts. Cover and let simmer gently for 15 minutes or until the chicken is cooked through and the apricots are tender.

Serving Suggestions:
Serve this apricot chicken with a side of steamed green beans or a quinoa salad for a balanced meal.

DINNER

Sardine Fish Cakes with Green Mix Salad

 SERVES 4   **PREP TIME** 20 MIN.   **COOK TIME** 10 MIN.

Ingredients:
2 cans of sardines in water
1 cup whole wheat breadcrumbs
1 large egg
2 tablespoons fresh parsley
1 tablespoon lemon juice
2 teaspoons Dijon mustard
1/2 teaspoon paprika
Salt and pepper, to taste
1 tablespoon olive oil
4 cups mixed greens
1/2 cucumber, sliced
1/2 red bell pepper, sliced
1/4 cup red onion, thinly sliced
2 tablespoons olive oil
1 tablespoon apple cider vinegar
1 teaspoon honey
Salt and pepper, to taste

> **Nutritional Information (Per Serving):**
> Calories: 320 kcal
> Protein: 20 g
> Carbohydrates: 20 g
> Fats: 18 g
> Fiber: 3 g
> Cholesterol: 100 mg
> Sodium: 450 mg
> Potassium: 450 mg

Directions:
In a large bowl, mash the sardines with a fork.Add whole wheat breadcrumbs, beaten egg, chopped parsley, lemon juice, Dijon mustard, paprika, salt, and pepper. Mix well until the ingredients are evenly combined.Form the mixture into eight small patties.
Heat olive oil in a non-stick skillet over medium heat.Cook the fish cakes on each side for 4-5 minutes or until golden and crispy. Set aside on a paper towel to drain any excess oil.
Combine mixed greens, cucumber slices, red bell pepper slices, and red onion in a large bowl.Whisk together olive oil, apple cider vinegar, honey, salt, and pepper in a small bowl to make the dressing.Toss the salad with the dressing before serving to keep the greens fresh and crisp.

Serving Suggestions:
Garnish with lemon wedges for an extra zing, and sprinkle a little flaxseed over the salad for added fiber.

Chicken Velouté

 SERVES 4   **PREP TIME** 15 MIN.   **COOK TIME** 25 MIN.

Ingredients:
2 tablespoons olive oil
4 boneless, skinless chicken breasts
2 tablespoons whole wheat flour
2 cups low-sodium chicken broth
1 cup skim milk
1 onion
2 cloves garlic
1 carrot
1 celery stalk
1 teaspoon dried thyme
Salt and pepper, to taste

> **Nutritional Information (Per Serving):**
> Calories: 250 kcal
> Protein: 28 g
> Carbohydrates: 14 g
> Fats: 9 g
> Fiber: 2 g
> Cholesterol: 65 mg
> Sodium: 220 mg
> Potassium: 450 mg

Directions:
Heat one tablespoon of olive oil in a large saucepan over medium heat.Add the cubed chicken and season with salt and pepper. Cook until browned and cooked through, about 5-7 minutes. Remove chicken from the pan and set aside.

Make the Roux:
In the same saucepan, add the remaining tablespoon of olive oil.
Stir in the whole wheat flour and cook for about 2 minutes, stirring constantly, to form a light roux.
Add the chopped onion, garlic, carrot, and celery to the roux. Cook until the vegetables are softened, about 5 minutes.
Gradually whisk in the chicken broth and skim milk, ensuring there are no lumps. Bring to a simmer.
Add the dried thyme and the cooked chicken back to the pan. Let the mixture simmer gently for about 15 minutes or until the sauce thickens and the flavors melde.

Serving Suggestions:
For a balanced meal, pair this velouté with a side of steamed green vegetables, such as broccoli or green beans, and a portion of whole-grain rice or quinoa.

DINNER

Mediterranean Turkey Stuffed

 SERVES 4 **PREP TIME** 15 MIN. **COOK TIME** 30 MIN.

Ingredients:
4 large bell peppers
1 tablespoon olive oil
1 onion
2 cloves garlic
1 pound ground turkey breast (lean)
1 cup cooked quinoa
1 cup chopped spinach
1/2 cup crumbled feta cheese (low-fat)
1/4 cup chopped fresh parsley
1/4 cup chopped fresh mint
1 teaspoon dried oregano
Salt and pepper, to taste
1 can (14 oz) diced tomatoes, no salt added

Nutritional Information (Per Serving):

Calories: 350 kcal

Protein: 28 g

Carbohydrates: 27 g

Fats: 15 g

Fiber: 6 g

Cholesterol: 60 mg

Sodium: 320 mg

Potassium: 750 mg

Directions:
Season the chicken breasts with salt and pepper.
Preheat your oven to 375°F (190°C).Arrange the bell peppers in a baking dish, cut-side up.
Heat olive oil in a skillet over medium heat. Add the onion and garlic, sautéing until the onion becomes translucent.Add the ground turkey, breaking it up with a spoon, and cook until browned.Stir in the cooked quinoa, spinach, half of the feta cheese, parsley, mint, oregano, and season with salt and pepper. Cook for an additional 2-3 minutes.Add about half of the diced tomatoes to the mixture, stirring until everything is well combined.
Spoon the turkey and quinoa mixture into each pepper, packing it down and mounding it slightly at the top.Pour the remaining diced tomatoes around the peppers in the dish.
Cover the dish with foil and bake for about 25-30 minutes. Remove the foil, sprinkle the remaining feta cheese over the peppers, and bake uncovered for another 5 minutes or until the cheese is slightly golden.

Serving Suggestions:
Pair with a side salad of mixed greens dressed with lemon and olive oil for a refreshing complement to the meal.

Chargrilled Turkey with Quinoa Tabbouleh & Tahini Dressing

SERVES 4 **PREP TIME** 20 MIN. **COOK TIME** 15 MIN.

Ingredients:
4 turkey breast cutlets
1 tablespoon olive oil
1 teaspoon garlic powder
1 teaspoon smoked paprika
Salt and pepper, to taste
1 cup quinoa
2 cups water
1 cup fresh parsley
1/2 cup fresh mint
1 cucumber
2 tomatoes
Juice of 1 lemon
2 tablespoons olive oil
Salt and pepper, to taste
1/4 cup tahini
1 garlic clove
Juice of 1/2 lemon
2 tablespoons water

Nutritional Information (Per Serving):

Calories: 490 kcal

Protein: 38 g

Carbohydrates: 38 g

Fats: 22 g

Fiber: 7 g

Cholesterol: 70 mg

Sodium: 300 mg

Potassium: 800 mg

Directions:
In a medium saucepan, bring 2 cups of water to a boil. Add the quinoa, reduce heat to low, cover, and simmer for about 15 minutes or until all water is absorbed. Remove from heat and let stand covered for 5 minutes. Fluff with a fork and let cool.Combine the cooked quinoa, chopped parsley, mint, cucumber, tomatoes, lemon juice, and two tablespoons of olive oil in a large bowl—season with salt and pepper to taste. Mix well and set aside to let flavors meld.Whisk together tahini, minced garlic, lemon juice, and water until smooth in a small bowl. Add salt to taste and adjust consistency with more water if needed.
Preheat a grill or grill pan over medium-high heat.Brush turkey cutlets with olive oil and season with garlic powder, smoked paprika, salt, and pepper.Grill each cutlet for 4-5 minutes on each side or until fully cooked and the internal temperature reaches 165°F (74°C).
Plate each grilled turkey cutlet with a generous serving of quinoa tabbouleh.Drizzle tahini dressing over the turkey and tabbouleh before serving.

Serving Suggestions:
Garnish with lemon wedges and additional fresh herbs if desired. Serve with steamed green beans or roasted vegetables for a complete meal.

DINNER

Chicken and Vegetable Rissoles

 SERVES 4 **PREP TIME** 20 MIN. **COOK TIME** 20 MIN.

Ingredients:

1 pound ground chicken breast (lean)
1 cup grated zucchini
1 cup grated carrot
1/2 cup finely chopped onion
2 cloves garli
1/4 cup whole wheat breadcrumbs
1 large egg
2 tablespoons chopped fresh parsley
1 teaspoon dried thyme
Salt and pepper, to taste
1 tablespoon olive oil for cooking

Nutritional Information (Per Serving):

Calories: 260 kcal

Protein: 28 g

Carbohydrates: 15 g

Fats: 10 g

Fiber: 3 g

Cholesterol: 100 mg

Sodium: 300 mg

Potassium: 650 mg

Directions:

In a large bowl, combine the ground chicken, grated zucchini, grated carrot, chopped onion, minced garlic, whole wheat breadcrumbs, beaten egg, chopped parsley, dried thyme, and optional chili flakes—season with salt and pepper.Mix thoroughly until all ingredients are well blended.
Divide the mixture into eight equal portions. Shape each portion into a flat patty.
Heat the olive oil in a large, non-stick skillet over medium heat.Place the rissoles in the skillet and cook for 4-5 minutes on each side until golden brown and cooked through. Ensure the internal temperature reaches 165°F (74°C).

Serving Suggestions:

Accompany with a side of mixed greens dressed with a vinaigrette or steamed broccoli and cauliflower.

Sumac Turkey-Stuffed Pittas

 SERVES 4 **PREP TIME** 20 MIN. **COOK TIME** 10 MIN.

Ingredients:

1 pound ground turkey breast (lean)
2 tablespoons olive oil
1 large onion
2 cloves garlic
2 teaspoons sumac
1 teaspoon smoked paprika
Salt and pepper, to taste
4 whole wheat pita breads
1 cup fresh spinach leaves
1/2 cucumber
1 tomato
1/4 cup low-fat Greek yogurt
1 tablespoon tahini
Juice of 1 lemon

Nutritional Information (Per Serving):

Calories: 380 kcal

Protein: 30 g

Carbohydrates: 35 g

Fats: 12 g

Fiber: 6 g

Cholesterol: 70 mg

Sodium: 320 mg

Potassium: 650 mg

Directions:

Heat one tablespoon of olive oil in a large skillet over medium heat.Add the onion and garlic and sauté until the onion is translucent.Add the ground turkey to the skillet. Break the turkey up with a spatula as it cooks.Season with sumac, I smoked paprika, salt, and pepper. Cook until the turkey is browned and fully cooked, about 5-7 minutes. Remove from heat.
Mix the Greek yogurt, tahini, and lemon juice in a small bowl until smooth-season with a pinch of salt. Set aside.
Toast the whole wheat pita breads lightly, then cut them open to create pockets.Spread a layer of the tahini-yogurt sauce inside each pitta.Stuff with cooked turkey, fresh spinach leaves, cucumber slices, and tomato slices.

Serving Suggestions:

Serve with a side of mixed greens or a simple cucumber salad dressed with lemon juice and olive oil.

SNACKS AND APPETIZERS

Cucumber Avocado Rolls Peppers

 SERVES 4   **PREP TIME** 15 MIN.   **COOK TIME** 30 MIN.

Ingredients:
2 large cucumbers
1 ripe avocado
1 carrot
1/2 red bell pepper
1/4 cup thinly sliced red onion
1 tablespoon lime juice
1 teaspoon rice vinegar
1/2 teaspoon salt
1/4 teaspoon black pepper
1 tablespoon sesame seeds

Nutritional Information (Per Serving):
Calories: 120
Protein: 2 g
Carbohydrates: 15 g
Fats: 7 g
Fiber: 4 g
Cholesterol: 0 mg
Sodium: 200 mg
Potassium: 487 mg

Directions:
Use a vegetable peel or mandolin slicer to slice the cucumbers lengthwise into thin strips. Aim for about 16 long strips in total. Lay the strips flat on paper towels to drain any excess moisture.

In a medium bowl, mash the avocado with lime juice, rice vinegar, salt, and pepper until smooth but still chunky. Gently stir in the julienned carrot, red bell pepper, and sliced red onion.

Take a cucumber strip and lay it flat on a clean surface. Spread a thin layer of the avocado mixture along the length of the cucumber strip. Roll the cucumber tightly around the filling. Secure with a toothpick if necessary. Repeat with remaining cucumber strips and filling.

If using, garnish with chopped cilantro and sesame seeds. Serve with hoisin sauce or low-sodium soy sauce for dipping.

Serving Suggestions:
Serve chilled as an appetizer or a refreshing snack. Pair with herbal tea or a fresh lime soda (unsweetened) for a complete light meal.

Avocado and Tomato Bruschetta

 SERVES 6   **PREP TIME** 10 MIN.   **COOK TIME** 5 MIN.

Ingredients:
1 whole grain baguette, sliced into 12 pieces
2 ripe avocados
2 large tomatoes
1/4 cup finely chopped red onion
2 tablespoons chopped fresh basil
1 clove garlic
2 tablespoons balsamic vinegar
1 tablespoon olive oil
1/4 teaspoon salt
1/4 teaspoon black pepper

Nutritional Information (Per Serving):
Calories: 180
Protein: 5 g
Carbohydrates: 20 g
Fats: 10 g
Fiber: 5 g
Cholesterol: 0 mg
Sodium: 200 mg
Potassium: 450 mg

Directions:
Preheat your oven to 400°F (200°C). Arrange the baguette slices on a baking sheet. Toast in the oven for about 5 minutes or until the edges are crisp but not too hard. Remove and allow to cool slightly.

Combine the diced tomatoes, chopped red onion, minced garlic, and chopped basil in a bowl. Whisk together the balsamic vinegar, olive oil, salt, and pepper in a separate small bowl. If using, add honey or agave syrup here. Pour this dressing over the tomato mixture and stir to combine.

Mash the avocados in a bowl, keeping the texture slightly chunky. Spread a generous layer of mashed avocado on each toasted bread slice.

Spoon the tomato mixture over the avocado layer on each bread slice. If desired, sprinkle with red pepper flakes for a bit of heat.

Serving Suggestions:
This dish is best served fresh as a light lunch or a healthy appetizer. Pair it with a side salad or clear soup for a complete meal.

SNACKS AND APPETIZERS

Caprese Salad Skewers Peppers

 SERVES 6   **PREP TIME** 10 MIN.   **COOK TIME** 30 MIN.

Ingredients:
24 cherry tomatoes
12 mini mozzarella balls
12 fresh basil leaves
2 tablespoons balsamic glaze
1 tablespoon olive oil
Salt and pepper to taste
12 wooden skewers

Nutritional Information (Per Serving):
Calories: 100
Protein: 8 g
Carbohydrates: 4 g
Fats: 6 g
Fiber: 1 g
Cholesterol: 10 mg
Sodium: 180 mg
Potassium: 150 mg

Directions:
Wash the cherry tomatoes and basil leaves gently under cold water. Pat them dry with a paper towel.
Thread one cherry tomato onto a skewer, followed by a basil leaf (fold it if it's significant), and then a mini mozzarella ball. Repeat the sequence with another tomato and basil leaf, and finish with a tomato.
Drizzle the skewers with olive oil and balsamic glaze (if using). To taste, sprinkle with salt, pepper, lemon zest, or red pepper flakes.

Serving Suggestions:
These skewers are perfect as a refreshing appetizer or a light snack. They can be paired with a quinoa salad or a lean protein-like grilled chicken for a more substantial meal.

Vegan Cauliflower Wings

 SERVES 4   **PREP TIME** 15 MIN.   **COOK TIME** 25 MIN.

Ingredients:
1 large head of cauliflower
1 cup unsweetened almond milk
3/4 cup whole wheat flour
1 teaspoon garlic powder
1 teaspoon onion powder
1/2 teaspoon paprika
1/2 teaspoon salt
1/4 teaspoon black pepper
 1/4 teaspoon cayenne pepper
1 cup low-sodium hot sauce
or barbecue sauce
1 tablespoon olive oil

Nutritional Information (Per Serving):
Calories: 180
Protein: 6 g
Carbohydrates: 28 g
Fats: 5 g
Fiber: 5 g
Cholesterol: 0 mg
Sodium: 600 mg (varies with the type of sauce used)
Potassium: 300 mg

Directions:
Preheat your oven to 450°F (230°C). Line a baking sheet with parchment paper.Wash the cauliflower florets and dry them thoroughly.
In a large bowl, mix the almond milk, flour, garlic powder, onion powder, paprika, salt, black pepper, and cayenne pepper (if using) until smooth.Dip each cauliflower floret into the batter, shaking off any excess. Place the battered florets on the prepared baking sheet in a single layer.
Bake for 20 minutes, turning halfway through, until the batter is hardened and slightly golden.
While the cauliflower is baking, mix the hot sauce with olive oil in a small saucepan and warm it over low heat, stirring occasionally.
Remove the cauliflower from the oven and gently toss them in the warm sauce. Then, please return them to the baking sheet and bake for 5 minutes to set the sauce.

Serving Suggestions:
Serve these cauliflower wings with celery sticks and a vegan ranch or blue cheese dressing.
Pair a fresh green salad or a quinoa pilaf for a complete meal.

SNACKS AND APPETIZERS

Guacamole with Pita Chips

 SERVES 4   **PREP TIME** 20 MIN.   **COOK TIME** 10 MIN.

Ingredients:

For the Guacamole:
3 ripe avocados
1 ripe tomato, finely chopped
1/4 cup finely chopped red onion
1 clove garlic
1 jalapeño, seeded and finely chopped
2 tablespoons freshly squeezed lime juice
1/4 teaspoon salt
Freshly ground black pepper

For the Pita Chips:
4 whole wheat pita breads
1 tablespoon olive oil
1/2 teaspoon garlic powder
1/2 teaspoon paprika
Salt, to taste

Nutritional Information (Per Serving):

Calories: 350

Protein: 6 g

Carbohydrates: 45 g

Fats: 18 g

Fiber: 10 g

Cholesterol: 0 mg

Sodium: 300 mg

Potassium: 850 mg

Directions:

Preheat your oven to 375°F (190°C).Cut the pita bread into eighths and separate the layers.Brush each piece lightly with olive oil and sprinkle with garlic powder, paprika, and a pinch of salt.Arrange the pita pieces in a single layer on a baking sheet.Bake for 8-10 minutes, until crispy and golden. Remove from the oven and let cool.

In a medium bowl, mash the avocados with a fork until they reach your desired consistency.Stir in the tomato, red onion, garlic, jalapeño (if using), and lime juice.Season with salt and pepper to taste. Mix thoroughly.

Transfer the guacamole to a serving bowl and garnish with chopped cilantro if desired.Serve with the cooled pita chips on the side.

Serving Suggestions:

Add fresh salsa or a bean salad for additional protein and fiber to enhance the meal.

Garden Hummus

 SERVES 6   **PREP TIME** 15 MIN.   **COOK TIME** 15 MIN.

Ingredients:

1 can chickpeas
1/4 cup low-fat, plain Greek yogurt
1/4 cup lemon juice
1 garlic clove
1/2 teaspoon salt
1/4 teaspoon black pepper
1 cup fresh spinach leaves
1/2 cup fresh parsley
1/2 cup grated carrot
1/2 cucumber

Nutritional Information (Per Serving):

Calories: 130

Protein: 6 g

Carbohydrates: 18 g

Fats: 3 g

Fiber: 5 g

Cholesterol: 0 mg

Sodium: 300 mg

Potassium: 250 mg

Directions:

Combine chickpeas, Greek yogurt, lemon juice, garlic, salt, and pepper in a food processor. Blend until smooth.

Add spinach and parsley to the chickpea mixture in the food processor. Blend again until the greens are well incorporated, and the hummus turns light green.

Transfer the hummus to a mixing bowl. Stir in the grated carrot and diced cucumber by hand to add texture and freshness.

Cover and refrigerate the hummus for about an hour to allow the flavors to meld together beautifully.

Spoon the hummus into a serving dish. Drizzle with a teaspoon of olive oil.

Serving Suggestions:

Serve this garden hummus with homemade whole wheat pita chips, fresh vegetable sticks, or a spread on whole grain wraps.

It's also excellent as part of a Mediterranean platter with olives, roasted peppers, and dolmas.

SNACKS AND APPETIZERS

No-Bake Blueberry Energy Bites

 SERVES 12   **PREP TIME** 15 MIN.   **COOK TIME** 30 MIN.

Ingredients:
1 cup rolled oats
1/2 cup fresh blueberries
1/4 cup ground flaxseed
1/4 cup unsweetened shredded coconut
1/4 cup natural peanut butter
1/4 cup honey or agave nectar
1 teaspoon vanilla extract
1 tablespoon chia seeds
1/4 teaspoon cinnamon

Nutritional Information (Per Serving):
Calories: 130
Protein: 3 g
Carbohydrates: 18 g
Fats: 6 g
Fiber: 3 g
Cholesterol: 0 mg
Sodium: 10 mg
Potassium: 120 mg

Directions:
Combine the rolled oats, ground flaxseed, shredded coconut, optional chia seeds, and cinnamon in a large bowl. Gently fold in the blueberries, being careful not to crush them.

In a small saucepan over low heat, warm the peanut butter and honey (or agave nectar) with the vanilla extract until they become easily stirrable. Pour the warm liquid over the oat mixture and stir until everything is well coated and sticks together.

Using your hands, form the mixture into 12 evenly-sized balls. Wet your hands slightly if the mixture is too sticky before forming the balls.

Place the energy bites on a baking sheet lined with parchment paper and refrigerate for at least 30 minutes to set.

Store the energy bites in an airtight container in the refrigerator for up to one week or freeze for more extended storage.

Serving Suggestions:
Enjoy these energy bites as a mid-morning snack, a pre-workout boost, or a healthy treat to satisfy sweet cravings.

Pair with a cup of herbal tea or almond milk for a balanced snack.

Pecan Granola Bars

 SERVES 12   **PREP TIME** 15 MIN.   **COOK TIME** 2 HOUR

Ingredients:
2 cups rolled oats
1/2 cup chopped pecans
1/4 cup ground flaxseed
1/4 cup sunflower seeds
1/4 cup unsweetened shredded coconut
1/4 cup dried cranberries (unsweetened)
1/4 cup honey or maple syrup
1/4 cup unsweetened applesauce
1 teaspoon vanilla extract
1/2 teaspoon ground cinnamon
1/4 teaspoon salt
1 tablespoon chia seeds

Nutritional Information (Per Serving):
Calories: 180
Protein: 4 g
Carbohydrates: 23 g
Fats: 9 g
Fiber: 4 g
Cholesterol: 0 mg
Sodium: 50 mg
Potassium: 150 mg

Directions:
Combine rolled oats, chopped pecans, ground flaxseed, sunflower seeds, shredded coconut, dried cranberries, and optional chia seeds in a large mixing bowl.

In a small saucepan over medium heat, gently warm the honey (or maple syrup), unsweetened applesauce, vanilla extract, cinnamon, and salt. Stir until the mixture is thoroughly combined and slightly liquid.

Pour the warm, wet ingredients over the dry ingredients in the bowl. Stir thoroughly until all the dry ingredients are evenly coated.

Line an 8x8-inch baking pan with parchment paper. Transfer the granola mixture to the pan, pressing it firmly into an even layer. The former you press, the better the bars will hold together.

Refrigerate the pan for at least 2 hours to allow the bars to set.

Remove the chilled mixture from the fridge, lift out of the pan using the edges of the parchment paper, and cut into 12 equal bars.

Serving Suggestions:
These granola bars are great for breakfast on the go or as a midday snack.

Pair with a low-fat yogurt or fresh fruit for a balanced snack.

SNACKS AND APPETIZERS

Herby Baked Falafel Bites with Spicy Mint Tahini Dip

 SERVES 6   **PREP TIME** 20 MIN.   **COOK TIME** 25 MIN.

Ingredients:

For the Falafel Bites:
2 cups canned chickpeas
1/4 cup chopped onion
2 cloves garlic
1/4 cup fresh parsley
1/4 cup fresh cilantro
2 tablespoons fresh dill
1 teaspoon ground cumin
1 teaspoon ground coriander
1/2 teaspoon salt
1/4 teaspoon black pepper
2 tablespoons whole wheat flour
1 teaspoon baking powder

For the Spicy Mint Tahini Dip:
1/4 cup tahini
1/4 cup water
1 tablespoon lemon juice
1 tablespoon fresh mint
1/2 teaspoon crushed red pepper flakes
Salt, to taste

> **Nutritional Information (Per Serving):**
> Calories: 210
> Protein: 8 g
> Carbohydrates: 27 g
> Fats: 8 g
> Fiber: 6 g
> Cholesterol: 0 mg
> Sodium: 300 mg
> Potassium: 350 mg

Directions:

Preheat your oven to 375°F (190°C). Line a baking sheet with parchment paper.In a food processor, combine the chickpeas, onion, garlic, parsley, cilantro, dill, cumin, coriander, salt, and pepper. Pulse until the mixture is finely ground but not pasty. Transfer to a bowl and stir in the whole wheat flour and baking powder until well combined. Let sit for 10 minutes to allow the mixture to firm up.

With damp hands, form the mixture into small balls or patties about 1 inch in diameter.Place on the prepared baking sheet and bake for 20-25 minutes, flipping halfway through, until golden and firm.

While the falafel is baking, whisk tahini, water, lemon juice, chopped mint, red pepper flakes, and salt until smooth. Adjust the consistency by adding more water if needed.

Serve the falafel bites warm with the spicy mint tahini dip.

Serving Suggestions:

These falafel bites can be served as an appetizer, as part of a meal with a side salad, or wrapped in whole wheat pita bread with fresh vegetables.

Air Fryer Everything Bagel Avocado Fries

 SERVES 4   **PREP TIME** 10 MIN. **COOK TIME** 8 MIN.

Ingredients:

2 large avocados, ripe but firm
1/2 cup almond flour
2 large eggs, beaten
1/2 cup panko breadcrumbs
(whole wheat for higher fiber)
2 tablespoons everything bagel seasoning
1/4 teaspoon garlic powder
1/4 teaspoon onion powder
Olive oil spray

> **Nutritional Information (Per Serving):**
> Calories: 280
> Protein: 8 g
> Carbohydrates: 23 g
> Fats: 19 g
> Fiber: 7 g
> Cholesterol: 93 mg
> Sodium: 300 mg
> Potassium: 487 mg

Directions:

Slice each avocado in half, remove the pit, and peel. Cut each half into 6 slices, resulting in 24 fries total.

Place almond flour in a shallow dish.Beat eggs in a second shallow dish.Mix panko breadcrumbs, bagel seasoning, garlic powder, and onion powder in a third shallow dish.

Dredge each avocado slice in the almond flour, shaking off excess.Dip next into the beaten eggs, allowing excess to drip off.Finally, coat thoroughly in the panko seasoning mix. Set aside on a plate.

Preheat the air fryer to 400°F (200°C).Spray the air fryer basket with olive oil spray. Place the breaded avocado slices in the basket in a single layer, ensuring they do not touch. Spray the tops with olive oil.Cook for about 8 minutes, flipping halfway through, until golden brown and crispy.

Serving Suggestions:

These avocado fries make an excellent snack or appetizer. They pair well with a yogurt-based dip or fresh salsa for added flavor.

SNACKS AND APPETIZERS

Steamed Edamame Recipe

 SERVES 4   **PREP TIME** 5 MIN.   **COOK TIME** 5 MIN.

Ingredients:
2 cups frozen edamame in the pod
1 teaspoon sea salt
1/4 teaspoon garlic powder
A squeeze of fresh lemon juice
Crushed red pepper flakes for garnish

> **Nutritional Information (Per Serving):**
> Calories: 100
> Protein: 9 g
> Carbohydrates: 9 g
> Fats: 4 g
> Fiber: 4 g
> Cholesterol: 0 mg
> Sodium: 300 mg
> Potassium: 400 mg

Directions:
Prepare Edamame:
Rinse the frozen edamame under cold water to remove any ice crystals.
Steam the Edamame:
Fill a pot with about two inches of water and boil.
Place the edamame in a steamer basket or insert it and set it over boiling water. Make sure the water does not touch the edamame.
Cover and steam for about 5 minutes or until the edamame is tender and bright green.
Season:
Transfer the steamed edamame to a serving bowl.
Sprinkle it with sea salt, garlic powder, and a squeeze of fresh lemon juice. Toss to coat evenly.

Serving Suggestions:
Enjoy this steamed edamame as a healthy appetizer or snack.
It can also be served as a side dish with Asian-inspired meals like stir-fry or sushi.
Pair with a low-sodium soy sauce or a homemade dipping sauce incorporating ginger and wasabi for additional flavor.

Cranberry Whipped Feta Dip

 SERVES 6   **PREP TIME** 10 MIN.   **COOK TIME** 20 MIN.

Ingredients:
1 cup low-fat feta cheese
1/2 cup low-fat cream cheese
1/2 cup fresh or frozen cranberries
1 tablespoon honey
1 tablespoon fresh orange juice
1 teaspoon orange zest
1/4 teaspoon salt
Freshly ground black pepper to taste

> **Nutritional Information (Per Serving):**
> Calories: 130
> Protein: 6 g
> Carbohydrates: 9 g
> Fats: 8 g
> Fiber: 0.5 g
> Cholesterol: 25 mg
> Sodium: 400 mg
> Potassium: 60 mg

Directions:
If using fresh cranberries, rinse and sort them (discard any soft or discolored ones). If using frozen cranberries, let them thaw first. Combine cranberries, honey (if using), and orange juice in a small saucepan. Cook over medium heat until the cranberries begin to burst, and the mixture thickens slightly about 5-7 minutes. Allow to cool completely.
In a food processor, blend the feta and cream cheese until smooth. Add the cooled cranberry mixture, orange zest, salt, and pepper. Process until the mixture is well combined and smooth.
For best flavor, cover and refrigerate the dip for at least 30 minutes before serving. This allows the flavors to meld together.

Serving Suggestions:
Serve this dip with a platter of fresh vegetables like cucumber slices, carrot sticks, and bell pepper strips.
It also pairs well with whole-grain pita chips or freshly baked whole-grain bread for dipping.
This dip can be a festive addition to holiday tables or a refreshing summer snack.

SNACKS AND APPETIZERS

Air Fryer Loaded Zucchini Skins

 SERVES 4   **PREP TIME** 15 MIN.   **COOK TIME** 10 MIN.

Ingredients:
4 medium zucchini, halved lengthwise
1/2 cup low-fat ricotta cheese
1/4 cup finely chopped red bell pepper
1/4 cup finely chopped onion
2 cloves garlic
1/2 cup canned black beans
1/2 teaspoon ground cumin
1/2 teaspoon paprika
1/4 teaspoon salt
1/4 teaspoon black pepper
Olive oil spray

Nutritional Information (Per Serving):

Calories: 150
Protein: 8 g
Carbohydrates: 20 g
Fats: 4 g
Fiber: 6 g
Cholesterol: 10 mg
Sodium: 200 mg
Potassium: 800 mg

Directions:
Scoop out the center of each zucchini half using a spoon or melon baller, leaving about 1/4 inch of zucchini along the shell. Chop the scooped-out zucchini flesh and set aside.
Preheat the air fryer to 375°F (190°C).Heat a non-stick skillet over medium heat. Spray lightly with olive oil spray. Add the chopped onion, bell pepper, and garlic, sautéing until soft, about 3-4 minutes.Add the chopped zucchini flesh, black beans, cumin, paprika, salt, and pepper. Cook for an additional 5 minutes, stirring occasionally.
Remove the skillet from heat. Let cool for a few minutes, then mix in the ricotta cheese.
Spoon the mixture back into the hollowed-out zucchini skins. Place the filled zucchini skins in the air fryer basket. Cook for 10 minutes or until the tops are golden and the zucchini is tender.
Garnish with fresh cilantro or parsley and a squeeze of lime if desired.

Serving Suggestions:
These loaded zucchini skins can be served as a nutritious appetizer, side dish, or light meal.
Pair with a fresh salad or a lean protein source for a balanced meal.

Beets with Feta and Pesto Sauce

 SERVES 4   **PREP TIME** 10 MIN.   **COOK TIME** 45 MIN.

Ingredients:
For the Roasted Beets:
4 medium beets
1 tablespoon olive oil
Salt and pepper, to taste
For the Low-Fat Pesto Sauce:
1 cup fresh basil leaves
2 cloves garlic
1/4 cup pine nuts or walnuts
2 tablespoons grated Parmesan cheese (low-fat)
1/4 cup olive oil

Nutritional Information (Per Serving):

Calories: 220
Protein: 6 g
Carbohydrates: 18 g
Fats: 14 g
Fiber: 5 g
Cholesterol: 8 mg
Sodium: 300 mg
Potassium: 400 mg

Directions:
Preheat your oven to 400°F (200°C).Toss the diced beets with 1 tablespoon of olive oil, salt, and pepper. Spread them on a baking sheet.Roast in the oven for about 45 minutes or until tender and slightly caramelized, stirring occasionally.
Combine basil leaves, garlic, nuts (if using), and Parmesan cheese in a food processor. Pulse until coarsely chopped.Add 1/4 cup of olive oil while processing until the pesto is smooth. Season with salt and pepper.
Mix the roasted beets with half of the pesto sauce in a serving bowl. Toss to coat evenly.
Plate the pesto-coated beets and sprinkle with crumbled feta cheese. Drizzle with the remaining pesto sauce and garnish with fresh basil leaves if desired.

Serving Suggestions:
This dish can be served warm or at room temperature as a side dish or as part of a vegetarian main course.
Pair it with a simple green salad or grilled chicken for a more substantial meal.

SNACKS AND APPETIZERS

Baba Ganoush

 SERVES 6   **PREP TIME** 10 MIN.   **COOK TIME** 45 MIN.

Ingredients:
2 large eggplants
3 tablespoons tahini
2 cloves garlic, minced
2 tablespoons lemon juice
1/2 teaspoon ground cumin
Salt to taste

Nutritional Information (Per Serving):

Calories: 80

Protein: 3 g

Carbohydrates: 10 g

Fats: 4 g

Fiber: 5 g

Cholesterol: 0 mg

Sodium: 50 mg

Potassium: 400 mg

Directions:
Preheat your oven to 400°F (200°C).Pierce the eggplants with a fork several times and place them on a baking sheet. Roast in the oven for about 45 minutes or until the skin is charred and the inside is tender. Turn the eggplants halfway through cooking for even charring.

Remove the eggplants from the oven and let them cool. Once cool enough to handle, peel off the skin and discard it. Drain any excess liquid from the eggplant flesh to avoid a watery dip.

Combine the roasted eggplant flesh, tahini, minced garlic, lemon juice, and cumin in a food processor. Blend until smooth. Season with salt to taste.

For the best flavor, transfer the babaganoush to a bowl, cover, and refrigerate for an hour to allow the flavors to meld.

Serving Suggestions:
Serve the babaganoush with a platter of fresh vegetables like cucumber slices, carrot sticks, and bell pepper strips for dipping.
It can also be enjoyed with whole grain pita bread or as a sandwich spread.

Warm Spinach and Artichoke Dip

 SERVES 6   **PREP TIME** 15 MIN.   **COOK TIME** 20 MIN.

Ingredients:
1 can artichoke hearts
2 cups fresh spinach
1 cup low-fat Greek yogurt
1/2 cup low-fat cream cheese
1/4 cup grated Parmesan cheese
2 cloves garlic
1/2 teaspoon salt
1/4 teaspoon black pepper

Nutritional Information (Per Serving):

Calories: 120

Protein: 8 g

Carbohydrates: 9 g

Fats: 5 g

Fiber: 2 g

Cholesterol: 15 mg

Sodium: 320 mg

Potassium: 200 mg

Directions:
Preheat your oven to 375°F (190°C).

If using fresh spinach, steam it in the microwave for 1-2 minutes until wilted, then squeeze out excess water.If using frozen spinach, thaw and drain thoroughly, pressing out as much liquid as possible.

In a large bowl, combine the chopped artichoke hearts, prepared spinach, Greek yogurt, cream cheese, Parmesan cheese, minced garlic, salt, and black pepper. Mix until well combined. If using, add lemon juice and red pepper flakes. Transfer the mixture to a baking dish (8x8 inch works well) and spread evenly.Bake in the preheated oven for 20 minutes or until hot and bubbly.

Serving Suggestions:
For a heartier meal, serve alongside grilled chicken or fish.

SNACKS AND APPETIZERS

Dip Sauce with Artichoke and Kale

 SERVES 6   **PREP TIME** 10 MIN.   **COOK TIME** 5 MIN.

Ingredients:
1 can artichoke hearts
2 cups kale
1 cup low-fat Greek yogurt
1/2 cup low-fat cream cheese
2 cloves garlic
1 tablespoon lemon juice
1/2 teaspoon salt
1/4 teaspoon black pepper

Nutritional Information (Per Serving):
Calories: 110
Protein: 7 g
Carbohydrates: 9 g
Fats: 4 g
Fiber: 3 g
Cholesterol: 10 mg
Sodium: 300 mg
Potassium: 200 mg

Directions:
Add the chopped kale with a splash of water in a large skillet over medium heat. Sauté until the kale is wilted and tender, about 3-4 minutes. Remove from heat and let cool.Chop the artichoke hearts into small pieces suitable for dipping. Combine the sautéed kale, chopped artichokes, Greek yogurt, cream cheese, minced garlic, lemon juice, salt, and black pepper in a mixing bowl. Mix well until all ingredients are evenly distributed. If using, add crushed red pepper flakes and nutritional yeast.
For a smoother texture, pulse the mixture in a food processor or blend with an immersion blender until you reach your desired consistency.
Cover and refrigerate the dip for at least 30 minutes to allow the flavors to meld together.

Serving Suggestions:
This dip is perfect for parties as a healthy option or a daily snack to increase vegetable and fiber intake.
It pairs well with raw vegetables like carrots, celery, and bell peppers, or for a heartier snack, with whole-grain toast points or baked tortilla chips.

White Bean and Baked Eggplant Hummus

 SERVES 4 **PREP TIME** 15 MIN.   **COOK TIME** 30 MIN.

Ingredients:
1 medium eggplant
1 can white beans, drained and rinsed
2 cloves garlic
2 tablespoons lemon juice
1 tablespoon tahini
1/2 teaspoon ground cumin
Salt and pepper to taste
Olive oil spray

Nutritional Information (Per Serving):
Calories: 120
Protein: 6 g
Carbohydrates: 18 g
Fats: 3 g (less if tahini is omitted)
Fiber: 5 g
Cholesterol: 0 mg
Sodium: 200 mg
Potassium: 300 mg

Directions:
Preheat your oven to 400°F (200°C).Cut the eggplant into cubes and place on a baking sheet. Lightly spray with olive oil and season with salt and pepper.Bake for 25-30 minutes or until the eggplant is soft and beginning to brown. Remove from the oven and allow to cool.
In a food processor, combine the roasted eggplant, white beans, garlic, lemon juice, tahini (if using), cumin, and smoked paprika (if using). Season with salt and pepper.Blend until smooth, scraping down the sides as needed to ensure even mixing.
Taste the hummus and adjust the seasoning if necessary, adding more lemon juice, salt, or spices as desired.
Cover and refrigerate the hummus for the best flavor for at least an hour to allow the flavors to meld.

Serving Suggestions:
This hummus is excellent as a spread on whole-grain sandwiches or wraps.
Serve as part of a Mediterranean-inspired appetizer platter with other dips like tzatziki and roasted red pepper dip.

SNACKS AND APPETIZERS

Grilled Shrimp with Tzatziki Sauce and Capers

 SERVES 4   **PREP TIME** 20 MIN   **COOK TIME** 10 MIN

Ingredients:

For the Grilled Shrimp:
1 pound large shrimp
2 cloves garlic
Juice of 1 lemon
2 tablespoons olive oil
1/2 teaspoon paprika
Salt and pepper, to taste

For the Tzatziki Sauce:
1 cup low-fat Greek yogurt
1 small cucumber
2 cloves garlic
1 tablespoon fresh dill
1 tablespoon lemon juice

Nutritional Information (Per Serving):

Calories: 220

Protein: 25 g

Carbohydrates: 8 g

Fats: 10 g

Fiber: 1 g

Cholesterol: 180 mg

Sodium: 420 mg

Potassium: 300 mg

Directions:

Combine minced garlic, lemon juice, olive oil, paprika, salt, and pepper in a bowl. Add the shrimp and toss to coat evenly.Cover and refrigerate for at least 30 minutes to marinate.
In another bowl, mix the low-fat Greek yogurt, grated cucumber, minced garlic, chopped dill, lemon juice, and season with salt and pepper to taste.Cover and refrigerate until ready to serve to let flavors blend.
Preheat your grill or grill pan to medium-high heat.Remove shrimp from the marinade and thread onto skewers (if using wooden skewers, soak them in water for 30 minutes beforehand to prevent burning).Grill shrimp on each side for 2-3 minutes until they are pink and opaque.

Serving Suggestions:

Serve the grilled shrimp with a side of fresh greens or a quinoa salad for a balanced meal.

Tuna and Avocado Tartare

 SERVES 4   **PREP TIME** 20 MIN   **COOK TIME** 30 MIN

Ingredients:

8 ounces fresh, sushi-grade tuna
1 large ripe avocado
1/4 cup finely chopped red onion
1 small cucumber
2 tablespoons chopped fresh cilantro
Juice of 1 lime
1 teaspoon sesame oil
1 tablespoon low-sodium soy sauce or tamari
Salt and pepper, to taste

Nutritional Information (Per Serving):

Calories: 200

Protein: 14 g

Carbohydrates: 9 g

Fats: 13 g

Fiber: 4 g

Cholesterol: 25 mg

Sodium: 200 mg

Potassium: 500 mg

Directions:

Ensure all ingredients are finely diced for uniformity and ease of eating.Combine the tuna, avocado, red onion, and cucumber in a medium mixing bowl.
Add the chopped cilantro, lime juice, sesame oil (if using), and soy sauce to the bowl. Gently fold the ingredients together to combine without mashing the avocado.Season with salt and pepper to taste. Add sriracha or chili sauce if a spicy flavor is desired.
Cover the bowl with plastic wrap and refrigerate for at least 30 minutes to allow the flavors to meld together and the mixture to chill thoroughly.
Serve the tartare in small bowls or glasses. Garnish with sesame seeds, a small dab of wasabi, or a side of seaweed salad for additional flavor and presentation.

Serving Suggestions:

For those not strictly adhering to a low-carbohydrate diet, it can also be served with whole-grain crackers or thinly sliced rye bread.

VEGETABLE

Low-Fat Ratatouille

 SERVES 6   **PREP TIME** 20 MIN.   **COOK TIME** 40 MIN.

Ingredients:
1 medium eggplant
2 zucchinis
2 yellow squash
1 bell pepper
1 large onion
3 cloves garlic
1 can crushed tomatoes
2 tablespoons tomato paste
1 teaspoon dried basil
1 teaspoon dried thyme
1/2 teaspoon dried oregano
Salt and pepper, to taste
Olive oil spray (for sautéing)

Nutritional Information (Per Serving):
Calories: 90
Protein: 4 g
Carbohydrates: 20 g
Fats: 1 g
Fiber: 6 g
Sodium: 300 mg
Potassium: 650 mg

Directions:
Wash and chop all vegetables into consistent sizes to ensure even cooking.

Spray a large pot or Dutch oven lightly with olive oil spray and heat over medium heat. Add the onions and garlic, sautéing until onions are translucent. Add the bell peppers and continue to cook for another 5 minutes.

Add eggplant, zucchini, and yellow squash to the pot. Cook for about 10 minutes, stirring occasionally, until the vegetables soften.

Stir in the crushed tomatoes and tomato paste. Add basil, thyme, oregano, salt, and pepper (and red pepper flakes). Mix well to combine all ingredients.

Reduce the heat to low and let the ratatouille simmer for about 20 minutes until all the vegetables are tender and the flavors meld together.

Serving Suggestions:
For a complete meal, serve this hearty ratatouille as a main dish with a side of whole-grain bread or as a topping over cooked quinoa or brown rice.

It can also be served as a side dish with grilled chicken or fish for a protein-rich meal.

Artichoke Stuffed with Green Peas, Carrots, and Potatoes

 SERVES 4   **PREP TIME** 30 MIN.   **COOK TIME** 40 MIN.

Ingredients:
4 large artichokes
1 cup green peas
2 medium carrots
1 large potato
1 onion
2 cloves garlic
1 lemon
2 tablespoons olive oil
Salt and pepper to taste

Nutritional Information (Per Serving):
Calories: 220
Protein: 6 g
Carbohydrates: 34 g
Fats: 7 g
Fiber: 10 g
Cholesterol: 0 mg
Sodium: 200 mg
Potassium: 850 mg

Directions:
Fill a large bowl with water and add half a lemon juice. Cut off the stems of the artichokes, peel them, and use them in the stuffing. Remove the top third and brutal outer leaves of each artichoke. If present, scoop out the fuzzy choke with a spoon. Place the prepared artichokes in lemon water to prevent browning.

In a large skillet, heat the olive oil over medium heat. Add the chopped onion and garlic, sautéing until soft and translucent. Add the diced carrots, potatoes, and artichoke stems. Cook until slightly softened, about 10 minutes. Add the green peas and cook for another 5 minutes—season with salt, pepper, and lemon zest. If using, add a splash of white wine and let it reduce for a few minutes.

Preheat your oven to 375°F (190°C). Remove the artichokes from the lemon water and pat dry. Spoon the vegetable mixture into the center and between the leaves of each artichoke.

Place the stuffed artichokes in a baking dish with water at the bottom to prevent sticking and steam them slightly. Cover with foil and bake for 30-40 minutes or until the artichokes are tender and the leaves pull away easily.

Serving Suggestions:
This dish can be served as a main course or a substantial side dish.

Pair with a simple salad or a lean protein source like grilled chicken or fish for a balanced meal.

VEGETABLE

Cauliflower Steak with Mushrooms & Cheese

 SERVES 4   **PREP TIME** 15 MIN   **COOK TIME** 20 MIN

Ingredients:
2 large heads of cauliflower
2 cups sliced mushrooms
1 medium onion
2 cloves garlic
1/2 cup low-fat shredded
mozzarella cheese
2 tablespoons olive oil
Salt and pepper, to taste

Nutritional Information (Per Serving):
Calories: 190
Protein: 8 g
Carbohydrates: 15 g
Fats: 11 g
Fiber: 5 g
Cholesterol: 10 mg
Sodium: 180 mg
Potassium: 870 mg

Directions:
Preheat your oven to 400°F (200°C).Remove the leaves and trim the stem of the cauliflower, leaving the core intact.Cut the cauliflower into 1-inch thick slices (steaks). Depending on the size, you should get about two steaks per head.
Heat one tablespoon of olive oil in a large oven-safe skillet over medium heat.Place the cauliflower steaks in the skillet and sear for 2-3 minutes on each side until golden brown.
Transfer the skillet to the oven and roast the cauliflower for about 15 minutes or until tender.
While the cauliflower is roasting, heat the remaining tablespoon of olive oil in another skillet.Add the sliced onions and cook until they start to soften.Add the garlic and mushrooms, seasoning with salt, pepper, and optional herbs. Cook until the mushrooms are soft and browned, about 8 minutes.
Remove the cauliflower steaks from the oven.Top each steak with the sautéed mushroom and onion mixture.Sprinkle it with low-fat mozzarella cheese.
Set the oven to broil and place the skillet back in the oven. Broil for 3-5 minutes or until the cheese is melted and slightly golden.

Serving Suggestions:
Serve these cauliflower steaks with quinoa or a fresh green salad as a main dish.

Steamed Artichokes

 SERVES 4   **PREP TIME** 10 MIN   **COOK TIME** 35 MIN

Ingredients:
4 large artichokes
1 lemon

Nutritional Information (Per Serving):
Calories: 60
Protein: 4 g
Carbohydrates: 13 g
Fiber: 6 g
Sodium: 120 mg
Potassium: 474 mg
Potassium: 500 mg

Directions:
Rinse the artichokes under cold water.Cut off the stem close to the base, and remove the small leaves at the bottom. Slice about an inch off the top of each artichoke to remove the thorny tips.Use kitchen shears to trim the thorny tips off the outer leaves.Rub a lemon half over the cut parts of the artichokes to prevent browning.
Fill a large pot with a few inches of water, add the lemon halves and optional fresh herbs, and insert a steaming basket.Place the artichokes in the steaming basket, stem-side up.Bring the water to a boil, then reduce heat to low, cover, and simmer for about 25-35 minutes, depending on the size of the artichokes. They are done when a leaf from the middle can be pulled off easily.
Once cooked, remove the artichokes from the steamer and let them cool slightly for handling.

Serving Suggestions:
Pair them with other steamed vegetables and a source of lean protein for a full meal.

VEGETABLE

Easy Zucchini Boats

 SERVES 4 **PREP TIME** 15 MIN. **COOK TIME** 30 MIN.

Ingredients:
4 medium zucchini
1 cup quinoa
1 cup cherry tomatoes
1/2 cup red bell pepper
1/2 cup yellow bell pepper
1/2 cup red onion
2 cloves garlic
1 cup spinach
1/4 cup fresh parsley
1/4 cup fresh basil
1/2 cup low-fat feta cheese
1 tablespoon olive oil
1 teaspoon dried oregano
1 teaspoon dried thyme
1/2 teaspoon salt
1/4 teaspoon black pepper
Lemon zest from 1 lemon

Juice of 1 lemon

Nutritional Information (Per Serving):

Nutritional Information (Per Serving)

Calories: 170

Protein: 6g

Carbohydrates: 28g

Fats: 5g

Fiber: 6g

Sodium: 270mg

Potassium: 800mg

Directions:
Preheat your oven to 375°F (190°C). Wash the zucchini thoroughly and cut them in half lengthwise. Using a spoon, scoop out the seeds and flesh to create a hollow center for the filling, leaving about 1/4-inch thick walls. Place the hollowed-out zucchini halves on a baking sheet lined with parchment paper. Rinse 1/2 cup of quinoa under cold water. Combine 1 cup of water with the quinoa in a saucepan. Bring to a boil, then reduce the heat to low, cover, and simmer for about 15 minutes until the water is absorbed and the quinoa is tender-fluff with a fork.

Combine the cooked quinoa, diced cherry tomatoes, red and yellow bell peppers, red onion, minced garlic, spinach, parsley, and basil in a large mixing bowl.

Add the olive oil, dried oregano, dried thyme, salt, black pepper, lemon zest, and lemon juice. Mix well to combine all ingredients.mIf using, gently fold in the crumbled feta cheese. Spoon the quinoa and vegetable mixture into the hollowed-out zucchini halves, pressing down gently to pack the filling. Place the filled zucchini boats in the oven and bake for 25-30 minutes until the zucchini is tender and the filling is heated.

Broccoli, Cauliflower, and Mushroom Casserole

 SERVES 6 **PREP TIME** 20 MIN. **COOK TIME** 35 MIN.

Ingredients:
2 cups broccoli florets
2 cups cauliflower florets
2 cups mushrooms
1 medium onion
3 cloves garlic
1 cup low-sodium vegetable broth
1 cup unsweetened almond milk
2 tablespoons whole wheat flour
2 tablespoons olive oil
1 teaspoon dried thyme
1 teaspoon dried oregano
1/2 teaspoon black pepper
1/4 teaspoon salt
1/4 cup nutritional yeast

Nutritional Information (Per Serving):

Calories: 140

Protein: 5g

Carbohydrates: 18g

Fats: 6g

Fiber: 4g

Cholesterol: 0mg

Sodium: 270mg

Potassium: 540mg

Directions:
Preheat your oven to 375°F (190°C).
Wash and cut the broccoli and cauliflower into small florets. Slice the mushrooms and finely chop the onion.Mince the garlic.Bring a large pot of water to a boil.Add the broccoli and cauliflower florets and blanch for 2-3 minutes until they are slightly tender but still crisp.Drain and transfer the florets to a bowl of ice water to stop the cooking process. Drain again and set aside.In a large saucepan, heat the olive oil over medium heat.Add the chopped onion, garlic, and sauté until the onion becomes translucent.Stir in the sliced mushrooms and cook until they release moisture and brown.Sprinkle the whole wheat flour over the vegetables, stirring constantly for about 1 minute to cook the flour.Gradually whisk in the vegetable broth and almond milk, continuing to whisk until the sauce thickens.Add the dried thyme, dried oregano, black pepper, and salt. Stir to combine.Add the nutritional yeast to the sauce for a cheesy flavor. Stir well. Gently fold the blanched broccoli and cauliflower into the sauce, ensuring they are well-coated.Transfer the vegetable and sauce mixture into a lightly greased 9x13-inch baking dish.If using, sprinkle the whole wheat bread crumbs evenly over the top of the casserole.Place the baking dish in the oven and bake for 25-30 minutes until the top is golden brown and the casserole is heated.

Serving Suggestions:
Pair it with a fresh green salad or a serving of whole grains like quinoa or brown rice for a balanced meal.

VEGETABLE

Broccoli Stir-Fry

 SERVES 4   **PREP TIME** 10 MIN.   **COOK TIME** 10 MIN.

Ingredients:
4 cups broccoli florets
1 medium red bell pepper
1 medium yellow bell pepper
1 medium carrot
1 cup snow peas
1 small red onion
3 cloves garlic
1 tablespoon fresh ginger
1/4 cup low-sodium vegetable broth
2 tablespoons low-sodium soy sauce
1 tablespoon rice vinegar
1 tablespoon sesame oil
1 tablespoon olive oil
1 teaspoon cornstarch mixed with 2 tablespoons water
1/4 teaspoon black pepper
1 tablespoon sesame seeds

2 tablespoons fresh cilantro

Nutritional Information (Per Serving):
Calories: 110
Protein: 4g
Carbohydrates: 15g
Fats: 5g
Fiber: 5g
Sodium: 290 mg
Potassium: 400mg

Directions:
Wash and cut the broccoli into small florets.Slice the red and yellow bell peppers.Julienne the carrot.Trim the snow peas. Thinly slice the red onion.Mince the garlic and fresh ginger.
Mix the low-sodium vegetable broth, soy sauce, rice vinegar, sesame oil, and the cornstarch slurry (cornstarch mixed with water) in a small bowl. Set aside.
Heat the olive oil in a large wok or skillet over medium-high heat.Add the minced garlic and ginger, and stir-fry for 30 seconds until fragrant.Add the red onion and stir-fry for about 2 minutes until it softens.Add the broccoli florets, red and yellow bell peppers, carrots, and snow peas. Stir-fry for about 5-6 minutes until the vegetables are tender-crisp.
Pour the prepared sauce over the vegetables in the wok.Stir well to coat the vegetables evenly.Cook for another 2 minutes, stirring frequently, until the sauce thickens slightly.

Serving Suggestions:
Serve this broccoli stir-fry over a bed of brown rice, quinoa, or cauliflower rice for a complete meal. It can also be paired with a lean protein source such as tofu, grilled chicken, or shrimp.

Crispy Brussels Sprouts with Balsamic Reduction

 SERVES 4   **PREP TIME** 10 MIN.   **COOK TIME** 25 MIN.

Ingredients:
1 lb (450g) Brussels sprouts
1 tablespoon olive oil
1/4 teaspoon salt
1/4 teaspoon black pepper
1/2 cup balsamic vinegar
1 tablespoon honey
1 tablespoon lemon juice
2 cloves garlic
2 tablespoons fresh parsley

Nutritional Information (Per Serving):
Calories: 90
Protein: 3g
Carbohydrates: 15g
Fats: 3g
Fiber: 4g
Sodium: 150mg
Potassium: 450mg

Directions:
Preheat your oven to 400°F (200°C).
Trim the ends of the Brussels sprouts and remove any yellow or damaged outer leaves.Cut the Brussels sprouts in half. Place the halved Brussels sprouts in a large bowl.Drizzle with olive oil, and sprinkle with salt and black pepper.Toss to coat evenly.Spread the Brussels sprouts in a single layer on a baking sheet lined with parchment paper.Roast in the oven for 20-25 minutes or until golden brown and crispy, stirring halfway through the cooking time.
While the Brussels sprouts are roasting, pour the balsamic vinegar into a small saucepan.Add the honey (if using) and minced garlic.Bring to a simmer over medium heat, then reduce the heat to low.Let the mixture simmer until it reduces by half and becomes syrupy for about 10-15 minutes.Remove from heat and stir in the lemon juice.
Remove from the oven once the Brussels sprouts are roasted to your liking.Drizzle the balsamic reduction.Toss to coat evenly.

Serving Suggestions:
Serve these crispy Brussels sprouts with grilled chicken, fish, or tofu as a side dish. They also pair well with a whole grain like quinoa or brown rice for a complete meal.

VEGETABLE

Balsamic Roasted Vegetablese

 SERVES 4　 **PREP TIME** 15 MIN.　 **COOK TIME** 30 MIN.

Ingredients:
2 cups broccoli florets
2 cups cauliflower florets
1 medium red bell pepper
1 medium yellow bell pepper
1 medium zucchini
1 medium red onion
1 cup cherry tomatoes
2 tablespoons olive oil
1/4 cup balsamic vinegar
1 tablespoon Dijon mustard
1 tablespoon honey
3 cloves garlic
1 teaspoon dried thyme
1 teaspoon dried oregano
1/4 teaspoon salt
1/4 teaspoon black pepper
2 tablespoons fresh parsley

Nutritional Information (Per Serving):
Calories: 130
Protein: 3g
Carbohydrates: 19g
Fats: 6g
Fiber: 5g
Cholesterol: 0mg
Sodium: 180mg
Potassium: 540mg

Directions:
Preheat your oven to 425°F (220°C).
Wash and cut the broccoli and cauliflower into small florets. Cut the red and yellow bell peppers into strips. Slice the zucchini. Cut the red onion into wedges. Halve the cherry tomatoes.
Whisk together the olive oil, balsamic vinegar, Dijon mustard, honey (if using), minced garlic, dried thyme, dried oregano, salt, and black pepper in a small bowl.
Place all the prepared vegetables in a large mixing bowl. Pour the balsamic marinade over the vegetables. Toss well to coat all the vegetables evenly.
Spread the marinated vegetables in a single layer on a baking sheet lined with parchment paper. Roast in the preheated oven for 25-30 minutes, stirring halfway through, until the vegetables are tender and slightly caramelized.

Serving Suggestions:
These balsamic roasted vegetables can be served as a side dish with grilled chicken, fish, or tofu. They also pair well with a whole grain like quinoa, brown rice, or farro for a complete meal.

Eggplant Casserole

 SERVES 4　 **PREP TIME** 20 MIN.　 **COOK TIME** 45 MIN.

Ingredients:
2 medium eggplants
1 medium red onion
2 cloves garlic
1 cup cherry tomatoes
1 cup tomato sauce (low-sodium)
1/2 cup quinoa
1/4 cup fresh basil
1/4 cup fresh parsley
1 teaspoon dried oregano
1 teaspoon dried thyme
1/2 teaspoon black pepper
1/4 teaspoon salt
2 tablespoons olive oil
1/4 cup low-fat feta cheese
1/4 cup whole wheat breadcrumbs
1/4 cup grated Parmesan cheese
1 tablespoon balsamic vinegar

Nutritional Information (Per Serving):
Calories: 190
Protein: 6g
Carbohydrates: 25g
Fats: 8g
Fiber: 7g
Cholesterol: 5mg
Sodium: 300mg
Potassium: 700mg

Directions:
Preheat your oven to 375°F (190°C).
Slice the eggplants into 1/4-inch rounds. Sprinkle the slices with a pinch of salt and let them sit for about 10 minutes to draw out excess moisture. Pat them dry with paper towels.
Rinse 1/4 cup of quinoa under cold water. Combine 1/2 cup of water with the quinoa in a saucepan. Bring to a boil, then reduce the heat to low, cover, and simmer for about 15 minutes, until the water is absorbed and the quinoa is tender-fluff with a fork. Heat one tablespoon of olive oil over medium heat in a large skillet. Add the chopped red onion and sauté until it becomes translucent. Add the minced garlic and cook for another minute until fragrant. Stir in the cherry tomatoes, tomato sauce, dried oregano, dried thyme, black pepper, and salt. Simmer for about 10 minutes until the sauce thickens slightly. Lightly grease a 9x13-inch baking dish with the remaining olive oil. Layer half of the eggplant slices at the bottom of the dish. Spread half of the tomato sauce mixture over the eggplant slices. Sprinkle half of the cooked quinoa and half of the fresh basil and parsley. Repeat the layers with the remaining eggplant slices, tomato sauce mixture, quinoa, basil, and parsley. Sprinkle the top with low-fat feta cheese, whole wheat breadcrumbs, and grated Parmesan cheese. Drizzle the top with balsamic vinegar.
Cover the baking dish with aluminum foil and bake in the oven for 30 minutes. Remove the foil and bake for 15 minutes until the eggplants are tender and the top is golden brown.

VEGETABLE

Brown Rice Congri

 SERVES 6   **PREP TIME** 15 MIN.   **COOK TIME** 45 MIN.

Ingredients:
1 cup brown rice
1 1/2 cups low-sodium vegetable broth
1 1/2 cups water
1 cup black beans, cooked and drained
1 medium green bell pepper
1 medium red bell pepper
1 medium red onion
3 cloves garlic
1 teaspoon ground cumin
1 teaspoon dried oregano
1/2 teaspoon smoked paprika
1/4 teaspoon black pepper
1/4 teaspoon salt
2 tablespoons olive oil
2 bay leaves
1 tablespoon apple cider vinegar
1/4 cup fresh cilantro

Lime wedges

Nutritional Information (Per Serving):
Calories: 180
Protein: 5g
Carbohydrates: 32g
Fats: 4g
Fiber: 6g
Sodium: 200mg
Potassium: 480mg

Directions:
Rinse the brown rice under cold water.Finely chop the green and red bell peppers and the red onion.Mince the garlic. Heat the olive oil over medium heat in a large pot or Dutch oven.Add the chopped green and red bell peppers and red onion. Sauté until the vegetables are soft, about 5 minutes. Add the minced garlic and cook for another 1-2 minutes until fragrant. Stir in the ground cumin, dried oregano, smoked paprika, black pepper, and salt. Cook for 1 minute to toast the spices.Add the rinsed brown rice to the pot, stirring well to coat the rice with the spices and vegetables. Add the low-sodium vegetable broth, water, and bay leaves to the pot. Stir well.Bring the mixture to a boil, then reduce the heat to low, cover, and simmer for about 35-40 minutes, or until the rice is tender and the liquid is absorbed. Once the rice is cooked, gently stir in the black beans and apple cider vinegar.Cover and cook for an additional 5 minutes to heat the beans through. Remove the bay leaves and discard them.Fluff the rice with a fork.Garnish with freshly chopped cilantro and serve with lime wedges if desired.

Serving Suggestions:
Serve this brown rice congri as a main dish or as a side to grilled vegetables, tofu, chicken, or fish. It pairs well with a simple green salad or steamed vegetables.

Brown Rice with Vegetables

 SERVES 4 **PREP TIME** 15 MIN.   **COOK TIME** 45 MIN.

Ingredients:
1 cup brown rice
2 cups low-sodium vegetable broth
1 tablespoon olive oil
1 medium red onion
2 cloves garlic
1 medium carrot
1 medium zucchini
1 red bell pepper
1 yellow bell pepper
1 cup broccoli florets
1 cup spinach
1 teaspoon ground cumin
1 teaspoon dried oregano
1/2 teaspoon black pepper
1/4 teaspoon salt
1/4 cup fresh parsley
1 tablespoon lemon juice

Nutritional Information (Per Serving):
Calories: 200
Protein: 5g
Carbohydrates: 35g
Fats: 4g
Fiber: 6g
Cholesterol: 0mg
Sodium: 220mg
Potassium: 550mg

Directions:
Rinse the brown rice under cold water.In a medium saucepan, bring the low-sodium vegetable broth to a boil.Add the brown rice, reduce the heat to low, cover, and simmer for about 40-45 minutes or until the rice is tender and the liquid is absorbed—fluff with a fork.While cooking the rice, finely chop the red onion, garlic, carrot, zucchini, red bell pepper, yellow bell pepper, and broccoli florets. Chop the spinach and set aside separately.In a large skillet, heat the olive oil over medium heat.Add the chopped red onion and sauté until it becomes translucent.Add the minced garlic and cook for another 1-2 minutes until fragrant.Add the diced carrot, zucchini, red bell pepper, yellow bell pepper, and broccoli. Cook for 5-7 minutes, stirring occasionally, until the vegetables are tender-crisp.Once the rice is cooked, add it to the skillet with the sautéed vegetables.Stir in the chopped spinach and cook for another 2-3 minutes until the spinach is wilted.Add the ground cumin, dried oregano, black pepper, and salt. Stir well to combine.Remove from heat and stir in the lemon juice.Garnish with freshly chopped parsley before serving.

Serving Suggestions:
Serve this brown rice with vegetables as a main dish or as a side to grilled chicken, fish, or tofu. For a complete meal, it pairs well with a simple green salad or a side of steamed vegetables.

VEGETABLE

Stuffed Acorn Squash with Mushrooms and Cranberries

 SERVES 4   **PREP TIME** 15 MIN.   **COOK TIME** 50 MIN.

Ingredients:
2 medium acorn squashes
1 tablespoon olive oil
1 medium red onion
3 cloves garlic
2 cups mushrooms
1 cup quinoa
1/2 cup dried cranberries
1/4 cup fresh parsley
1 teaspoon dried thyme
1 teaspoon dried rosemary
1/4 teaspoon black pepper
1/4 teaspoon salt
1/4 cup low-sodium vegetable broth

1 tablespoon balsamic vinegar

Nutritional Information (Per Serving):

Calories: 250

Protein: 6g

Carbohydrates: 46g

Fats: 5g

Fiber: 8g

Sodium: 180mg

Potassium: 800m

Directions:
Preheat your oven to 400°F (200°C).
Cut the acorn squashes in half lengthwise and scoop out the seeds.Place the squash halves cut-side down on a baking sheet lined with parchment paper.Bake in the preheated oven for 35-40 minutes or until the flesh is tender and easily pierced with a fork. Rinse 1/2 cup of quinoa under cold water. Combine 1 cup of water with the quinoa in a saucepan. Bring to a boil, then reduce the heat to low, cover, and simmer for about 15 minutes until the water is absorbed and the quinoa is tender—fluff with a fork. In a large skillet, heat the olive oil over medium heat.Add the chopped red onion and sauté until it becomes translucent.Add the minced garlic and cook for another 1-2 minutes until fragrant.Stir in the sliced mushrooms and cook until they release moisture and brown.Add the cooked quinoa, cranberries, thyme, rosemary, black pepper, and salt. Mix well.Pour in the low-sodium vegetable broth and balsamic vinegar. Stir to combine and cook for another 2-3 minutes until the mixture is heated and well combined. Remove from heat and stir in the chopped fresh parsley. Once the acorn squash halves are tender, remove them from the oven and let them cool slightly.Fill each squash half with the mushroom and quinoa mixture, packing it down gently. Place the stuffed squash halves back on the baking sheet and bake for 10 minutes or until the filling is heated.

Serving Suggestions:
Serve the stuffed acorn squash as a main dish. Pair it with a side salad or steamed vegetables for a balanced meal.

Aloo Gobi (Potatoes and Cauliflower)

 SERVES 4   **PREP TIME** 15 MIN.   **COOK TIME** 30 MIN.

Ingredients:
2 medium potatoes
1 medium head of cauliflower
1 medium onion
2 cloves garlic
1-inch piece of ginger
2 medium tomatoes
1 tablespoon olive oil
1 teaspoon cumin seeds
1 teaspoon ground turmeric
1 teaspoon ground coriander
1/2 teaspoon ground cumin
1/2 teaspoon ground paprika
1/4 teaspoon ground cayenne pepper
1/4 teaspoon black pepper
1/4 teaspoon salt
1/2 cup low-sodium vegetable broth
1/4 cup fresh cilantro
1 tablespoon lemon juice

Nutritional Information (Per Serving):

Calories: 180

Protein: 4g

Carbohydrates: 35g

Fats: 4g

Fiber: 7g

Sodium: 200mg

Potassium: 850mg

Directions:
Peel and dice the potatoes.Cut the cauliflower into florets. Finely chop the onion, tomatoes, garlic, and ginger.
Heat the olive oil over medium heat in a large skillet or pot.Add the cumin seeds and toast for about 1 minute until fragrant.Add the chopped onion, garlic, and ginger. Sauté for about 5 minutes until the onion becomes translucent.
Stir in the ground turmeric, ground coriander, ground cumin, ground paprika, and ground cayenne pepper (if using). Cook for about 1 minute, stirring continuously.
Add the diced potatoes and cauliflower florets to the skillet. Stir well to coat the vegetables with the spice mixture.Add the chopped tomatoes and low-sodium vegetable broth. Stir to combine.Cover the skillet and cook for about 20-25 minutes, stirring occasionally, until the potatoes and cauliflower are tender.
Once the vegetables are cooked, remove the lid and cook for 5 minutes to allow any excess liquid to evaporate.Stir in the lemon juice and adjust the seasoning with salt and black pepper to taste.Garnish with freshly chopped cilantro.

Serving Suggestions:
Serve the Aloo Gobi as a main dish with brown rice or quinoa or as a side dish with grilled chicken or tofu. It pairs well with a simple green salad or steamed vegetables.

VEGETABLE

Sautéed Eggplant

 SERVES 4 **PREP TIME** 15 MIN. **COOK TIME** 20 MIN.

Ingredients:
1 large eggplant
1 medium red onion
2 cloves garlic
1 red bell pepper
1 cup cherry tomatoes
2 tablespoons olive oil
1 teaspoon dried oregano
1 teaspoon dried basil
1/4 teaspoon black pepper
1/4 teaspoon salt
1 tablespoon balsamic vinegar
1/4 cup fresh parsley
1 tablespoon lemon juice

Nutritional Information (Per Serving):

Calories: 120

Protein: 2g

Carbohydrates: 15g

Fats: 7g

Fiber: 6g

Cholesterol: 0mg

Sodium: 180mg

Potassium: 500mg

Directions:
Cut the eggplant into 1-inch cubes.Place the eggplant cubes in a colander, sprinkle with a pinch of salt, and let them sit for 10 minutes to draw out excess moisture. Pat dry with paper towels.

Heat one tablespoon of olive oil over medium heat in a large skillet.Add the finely chopped red onion and sauté until it becomes translucent, about 5 minutes.Add the minced garlic and cook for another 1-2 minutes until fragrant.

Add the remaining one tablespoon of olive oil to the skillet. Add the cubed eggplant and cook for about 10 minutes, stirring occasionally, until tender and golden brown.

Stir in the diced red bell pepper and halved cherry tomatoes. Cook for an additional 5 minutes until the vegetables are tender.Add the dried oregano, dried basil, black pepper, and salt. Stir well to combine.

Remove the skillet from the heat and stir in the balsamic vinegar and lemon juice.Garnish with freshly chopped parsley before serving.

Serving Suggestions:
Serve the sautéed eggplant as a side dish with grilled chicken, fish, or tofu. For a complete meal, it pairs well with whole grains like quinoa or brown rice.

Fennel and Orange Salad with Walnuts

 SERVES 4 **PREP TIME** 15 MIN. **COOK TIME** 25 MIN.

Ingredients:
2 medium fennel bulbs
2 large oranges
1/4 cup walnuts
1/4 cup fresh mint leaves
1 tablespoon olive oil
1 tablespoon fresh lemon juice
1 teaspoon honey
1/4 teaspoon salt
1/4 teaspoon black pepper

Nutritional Information (Per Serving):

Calories: 130

Protein: 2g

Carbohydrates: 16g

Fats: 7g

Fiber: 4g

Cholesterol: 0mg

Sodium: 150mg

Potassium: 420mg

Directions:
Trim the fennel bulbs, removing the stalks and any tough outer layers.Slice the fennel bulbs thinly using a mandoline or sharp knife.

Peel the oranges and segment them, removing any seeds and membranes.Cut the segments into bite-sized pieces if desired.

Toast the walnuts in a dry skillet over medium heat for 3-5 minutes, stirring frequently, until they are lightly browned and fragrant.Remove from heat and let them cool, then chop roughly.

In a small bowl, whisk together the olive oil, fresh lemon juice, honey (if using), salt, and black pepper until well combined.

Combine the sliced fennel, orange segments, chopped walnuts, and fresh mint leaves in a large salad bowl.Drizzle the dressing over the salad and toss gently to combine all the ingredients evenly.

Serving Suggestions:
This fennel and orange salad with walnuts is a refreshing side dish for grilled chicken, fish, or tofu. It also pairs well with other Mediterranean-inspired dishes or as a light starter.

VEGETABLE

Avocado and Tomato Gazpacho

 SERVES 4   **PREP TIME** 15 MIN.   **COOK TIME** 20 MIN.

Ingredients:
4 large ripe tomatoes
1 medium cucumber
1 red bell pepper
1 small red onion
2 cloves garlic
1 medium avocado
2 cups low-sodium vegetable broth
2 tablespoons olive oil
2 tablespoons red wine vinegar
1 tablespoon fresh lime juice
1/4 teaspoon salt
1/4 teaspoon black pepper
1/4 cup fresh cilantro
1/4 cup fresh basil

> **Nutritional Information (Per Serving):**
> Calories: 180
> Protein: 3g
> Carbohydrates: 20g
> Fats: 12g
> Fiber: 6g
> Sodium: 220mg
> Potassium: 800mg

Directions:
Chop the tomatoes, cucumber, red bell pepper, red onion, and avocado.Mince the garlic.
Combine the chopped tomatoes, cucumber, red bell pepper, red onion, garlic, and avocado in a blender or food processor.Add the low-sodium vegetable broth, olive oil, red wine vinegar, lime juice, salt, and black pepper.Blend until smooth. If you prefer a chunkier texture, pulse the blender a few times instead of blending until completely smooth.
Transfer the gazpacho to a large bowl or pitcher.Cover and refrigerate for at least 1 hour to allow the flavors to meld and the soup to chill.
Stir the gazpacho well before serving.Ladle the gazpacho into bowls and garnish with freshly chopped cilantro and basil.

Serving Suggestions:
Serve this avocado and tomato gazpacho as a refreshing starter or a light main dish. It pairs well with a simple green salad or whole-grain crackers for added texture.

Spaghetti Squash with Tomato and Basil Sauce

SERVES 4   **PREP TIME** 15 MIN.   **COOK TIME** 45 MIN.

Ingredients:
1 large spaghetti squash
1 tablespoon olive oil
1 medium onion
3 cloves garlic
4 large tomatoes
1/4 cup tomato paste (low-sodium)
1/2 teaspoon dried oregano
1/2 teaspoon dried basil
1/4 teaspoon red pepper flakes
1/4 teaspoon salt
1/4 teaspoon black pepper
1/2 cup fresh basil
1/4 cup fresh parsley
1 tablespoon balsamic vinegar

> **Nutritional Information (Per Serving):**
> Calories: 180
> Protein: 4g
> Carbohydrates: 28g
> Fats: 5g
> Fiber: 7g
> Sodium: 220mg
> Potassium: 900mg

Directions:
Preheat your oven to 400°F (200°C).Cut the squash in half lengthwise and scoop out the seeds.Place the squash halves cut-side down on a baking sheet lined with parchment paper.Bake in the preheated oven for 35-40 minutes or until the flesh is tender and easily shredded with a fork.Once cooked, let it cool slightly, then use a fork to scrape out the spaghetti-like strands into a large bowl.
While the squash is baking, heat the olive oil in a large skillet over medium heat.Add the finely chopped onion and sauté until it becomes translucent, about 5 minutes.Add the minced garlic and cook for another 1-2 minutes until fragrant.Stir in the chopped tomatoes, tomato paste, dried oregano, dried basil, red pepper flakes (if using), salt, and black pepper. Reduce the heat to low and let the sauce simmer for 15-20 minutes, stirring occasionally, until it thickens and the flavors meld.
Stir the fresh basil and parsley into the tomato sauce.Add the balsamic vinegar and stir well to combine.Pour the tomato and basil sauce over the cooked spaghetti squash strands and toss gently to coat evenly.

Serving Suggestions:
Serve spaghetti squash with tomato and basil sauce as a main dish. For a balanced meal, it pairs well with a simple green salad or steamed vegetables.

VEGETABLE

Pumpkin Coconut Curry

 SERVES 4　 **PREP TIME** 15 MIN.　 **COOK TIME** 30 MIN.

Ingredients:

1 tablespoon olive oil
1 medium onion
3 cloves garlic
1-inch piece of ginger
2 cups pumpkin
1 red bell pepper
1 cup canned chickpeas
1 can light coconut milk
1 cup low-sodium vegetable broth
2 tablespoons red curry paste
1 teaspoon ground turmeric
1 teaspoon ground cumin
1/2 teaspoon ground coriander
1/4 teaspoon black pepper
1/4 teaspoon salt
1 cup spinach
1/4 cup fresh cilantro
1 tablespoon fresh lime juice

Nutritional Information (Per Serving):

Calories: 260

Protein: 6g

Carbohydrates: 36g

Fats: 10g

Fiber: 8g

Cholesterol: 0mg

Sodium: 300mg

Potassium: 700mg

Directions:

Peel and dice the pumpkin into 1-inch cubes.Finely chop the onion, red bell pepper, garlic, and ginger.
In a large pot, heat the olive oil over medium heat.Add the chopped onion and sauté until it becomes translucent, about 5 minutes.Add the minced garlic and ginger and cook for another 1-2 minutes until fragrant.
Stir in the diced pumpkin and red bell pepper. Cook for about 5 minutes, stirring occasionally.Add the red curry paste, turmeric, ground cumin, coriander, black pepper, and salt. Stir well to coat the vegetables with the spices.
Pour in the light coconut milk and low-sodium vegetable broth. Stir to combine.Add the canned chickpeas.Bring the mixture to a boil, then reduce the heat to low and simmer for about 20 minutes or until the pumpkin is tender.
Stir in the chopped spinach and cook for another 2-3 minutes until wilted.Remove from heat and stir in the fresh lime juice.

Serving Suggestions:

For a complete meal, serve this pumpkin coconut curry over brown rice, quinoa, or cauliflower rice. It pairs well with stea-med vegetables or a simple green salad.

83

DESSERTS

Baked Apples with Cinnamon and Honey

 SERVES 4   **PREP TIME** 15 MIN.   **COOK TIME** 40 MIN.

Ingredients:
4 medium apples
4 teaspoons honey
1 teaspoon ground cinnamon
1 teaspoon vanilla extract
1/4 cup old-fashioned oats
2 tablespoons chopped walnuts
2 tablespoons raisins or dried cranberries
1/4 cup water

Nutritional Information (Per Serving):

Calories: 152
Protein: 1.2g
Carbohydrates: 37g
Fats: 1.2g
Fiber: 4.5g
Cholesterol: 0mg
Sodium: 2mg
Potassium: 225m

Directions:
Preheat your oven to 350°F (175°C).
Wash and core the apples, leaving the bottom intact to hold the filling.
Combine the honey, ground cinnamon, vanilla extract, oats, and optional ingredients (walnuts and raisins or dried cranberries) in a small bowl. Stir well to create a uniform mixture. Evenly divide the filling mixture among the four cored apples. Place the apples in a baking dish.
Pour the 1/4 cup of water into the bottom of the baking dish. This helps to steam the apples, keeping them moist and preventing them from drying out.
Cover the baking dish with aluminum foil. Bake in the preheated oven for 30 minutes. Remove the foil and bake for 10 minutes, or until the apples are tender and the filling is golden brown.

Serving Suggestions:
Serve the baked apples warm as a dessert or a wholesome snack.

Berry Parfait with Greek Yogurt and Honey

 SERVES 4   **PREP TIME** 15 MIN.   **COOK TIME** 30 MIN.

Ingredients:
2 cups low-fat Greek yogurt
1 cup mixed berries
4 teaspoons honey
1 teaspoon vanilla extract
1/2 cup granola
2 tablespoons chia seeds
Fresh mint leaves

Nutritional Information (Per Serving):

Calories: 195
Protein: 10g
Carbohydrates: 31g
Fats: 3.5g
Fiber: 5g
Cholesterol: 5mg
Sodium: 55mg
Potassium: 350mg

Directions:
Wash the berries thoroughly. If using strawberries, hull and slice them.
Combine the low-fat Greek yogurt with the vanilla extract in a medium bowl. Stir until well mixed.
In 4 serving glasses or bowls, start with a layer of Greek yogurt. Add a layer of mixed berries on top of the yogurt. Drizzle one teaspoon of honey over the berries in each glass. Sprinkle a layer of granola over the berries and honey. Sprinkle 1/2 tablespoon of chia seeds on top of the granola for added fiber and omega-3.
Repeat the layers (yogurt, berries, honey, granola) until all ingredients are used up, ending with a layer of berries and a final drizzle of honey.
Chill the parfaits in the refrig

Serving Suggestions:
Enjoy the berry parfaits as a nutritious breakfast, snack, or dessert.
Pair with a warm cup of herbal tea for a soothing complement.

DESSERTS

Oatmeal and Banana Cookies

 SERVES 12 COOKES   **PREP TIME** 15 MIN.   **COOK TIME** 15 MIN.

Ingredients:
2 ripe bananas
1 1/2 cups old-fashioned oats
1/2 teaspoon ground cinnamon
1/2 teaspoon vanilla extract
1/4 cup raisins or dried cranberries
2 tablespoons chopped walnuts
1 tablespoon honey
1/4 teaspoon baking powder

Nutritional Information (Per Serving):

Calories: 70

Protein: 1.5g

Carbohydrates: 15g

Fats: 1g

Fiber: 2g

Sodium: 2mg

Potassium: 105mg

Directions:
Preheat your oven to 350°F (175°C). Line a baking sheet with parchment paper.
In a large bowl, mash the ripe bananas until smooth. Add the vanilla extract and optional honey. Mix well to combine.
Mix the old-fashioned oats, ground cinnamon, baking powder, and optional ingredients (raisins or dried cranberries and chopped walnuts) in a separate bowl.
Gradually add the dry and wet ingredients, stirring until thoroughly combined. The mixture should be thick and sticky.
Using a spoon or your hands, form small balls of dough (about 1-2 tablespoons each) and place them onto the prepared baking sheet. Flatten each ball slightly to form a cookie shape.
Bake in the preheated oven for 12-15 minutes or until the edges are golden brown and the cookies are set.

Serving Suggestions:
Enjoy the cookies as a healthy snack or a quick breakfast option.
Pair with a cup of green tea or a glass of almond milk for a nutritious treat.

Carrot Cake Muffins with Cream Cheese Frosting

 SERVES 12 MUFFINS   **PREP TIME** 20 MIN.   **COOK TIME** 25 MIN.

Ingredients:
Muffins:
1 cup whole wheat flour
1 cup finely grated carrots
1/2 cup old-fashioned oats
1/2 cup unsweetened applesauce
1/4 cup honey or maple syrup
2 large eggs
1/4 cup Greek yogurt
1 teaspoon vanilla extract
1 teaspoon ground cinnamon
1/2 teaspoon ground nutmeg
1/2 teaspoon baking soda
1 teaspoon baking powder
1/4 teaspoon salt
1/4 cup chopped walnuts or pecans
1/4 cup raisins or chopped dates
Cream Cheese Frosting:
4 ounces low-fat cream cheese
1/4 cup Greek yogurt
2 tablespoons honey or maple syrup
1/2 teaspoon vanilla extract

Nutritional Information (Per Serving):

Calories: 150

Protein: 4g

Carbohydrates: 25g

Fats: 4g

Fiber: 3g

Cholesterol: 30mg

Sodium: 190 mg

Potassium: 160mg

Directions:
Preheat your oven to 350°F (175°C). Line a muffin tin with paper liners or lightly grease with cooking spray.
In a large bowl, beat the eggs. Add the unsweetened applesauce, Greek yogurt, honey or maple syrup, and vanilla extract. Mix until well combined. Whisk together the whole wheat flour, old-fashioned oats, ground cinnamon, ground nutmeg, baking soda, baking powder, and salt in a separate bowl. Gradually add the dry ingredients to the wet ingredients, stirring until combined. Do not overmix. Fold the grated carrots and optional ingredients (chopped walnuts or pecans, raisins, or chopped dates). Evenly distribute the batter among the 12 muffin cups, filling each about two-thirds full. Bake in the preheated oven for 20-25 minutes or until a toothpick inserted into the center of a muffin comes out clean. Allow the muffins to cool in the tin for 5 minutes, then transfer to a wire rack to cool completely.
In a medium bowl, beat the softened cream cheese, Greek yogurt, honey or maple syrup, and vanilla extract until smooth and creamy. For a firmer frosting, chill in the refrigerator for 30 minutes before applying to the muffins.

DESSERTS

Chia Seed Pudding with Mango and Coconut

 SERVES 4   **PREP TIME** 10 MIN.   **COOK TIME** 20 MIN.

Ingredients:
1/2 cup chia seeds
2 cups unsweetened almond milk
2 tablespoons honey or maple syrup
1 teaspoon vanilla extract
1 large ripe mango
1/4 cup unsweetened shredded coconut
Fresh mint leaves

> **Nutritional Information (Per Serving):**
> Calories: 180
> Protein: 4g
> Carbohydrates: 28g
> Fats: 7g
> Fiber: 10g
> Sodium: 60mg
> Potassium: 250mg

Directions:
Combine the chia seeds, unsweetened almond milk, honey or maple syrup, and vanilla extract in a medium bowl. Stir well to ensure the chia seeds are evenly distributed.

Cover the bowl and refrigerate for at least 4 hours, preferably overnight. Stir the mixture once or twice during the first hour to prevent clumping.

While the chia pudding is chilling, peel and dice the mango into small cubes. Toast the shredded coconut in a dry skillet over medium heat for 2-3 minutes, stirring frequently until golden brown. Be careful not to burn it.

Once the chia pudding has been set, divide it evenly among four serving bowls or glasses. Top each serving with a portion of diced mango and a sprinkle of toasted coconut.

Serving Suggestions:
Enjoy the chia seed pudding as a nutritious breakfast, snack, or dessert.

Pair with a cup of green tea for a refreshing and healthy combination.

Dark Chocolate Avocado Mousse

 SERVES 4   **PREP TIME** 10 MIN.   **COOK TIME** 30 MIN.

Ingredients:
2 ripe avocados
1/4 cup unsweetened cocoa powder
1/4 cup honey or maple syrup
1/4 cup unsweetened almond milk
1 teaspoon vanilla extract
1/8 teaspoon salt
Fresh berries or mint leaves

> **Nutritional Information (Per Serving):**
> Calories: 180
> Protein: 3g
> Carbohydrates: 24g
> Fats: 10g
> Fiber: 7g
> Sodium: 60mg
> Potassium: 450mg

Directions:
Cut the avocados in half, remove the pits, and scoop the flesh into a food processor or blender.

Add the unsweetened cocoa powder, honey or maple syrup, almond milk, vanilla extract, and salt to the food processor or blender.

Blend the mixture until smooth and creamy, scraping down the sides as needed to ensure all ingredients are well combined.

Transfer the mousse to a bowl, cover, and refrigerate for at least 30 minutes to allow the flavors to meld and the mousse to firm up.

Divide the mousse into four serving dishes. Garnish with fresh berries or mint leaves if desired.

Serving Suggestions:
Serve the dark chocolate avocado mousse as a healthy dessert or a decadent snack.

Pair with a cup of herbal tea for a delightful and nutritious treat.

DESSERTS

Fresh Fruit Salad with Mint

 SERVES 4   **PREP TIME** 15 MIN.   **COOK TIME** 30 MIN.

Ingredients:
1 cup strawberries
1 cup blueberries
1 cup pineapple
1 cup kiwi
1 cup mango
2 tablespoons fresh mint leaves
1 tablespoon lime juice
1 tablespoon honey or maple syrup

Nutritional Information
(Per Serving):

Calories: 90

Protein: 1.5g

Carbohydrates: 22g

Fats: 0.5g

Fiber: 4g

Sodium: 5mg

Potassium: 240mg

Directions:
Wash all the fruits thoroughly.Hull and slice the strawberries. Dice the pineapple and mango.Peel and slice the kiwi. Combine the strawberries, blueberries, pineapple, kiwi, and mango in a large bowl.
Sprinkle the chopped fresh mint leaves over the fruit.In a small bowl, mix the lime juice and honey or maple syrup (if using). Drizzle this mixture over the fruit salad.
Gently toss the fruit salad to combine all the ingredients and coat the fruit with the lime juice mixture.For best results, cover and chill the fruit salad in the refrigerator for 30 minutes before serving to allow the flavors to meld.

Serving Suggestions:
Enjoy the fresh fruit salad as a refreshing breakfast, snack, or dessert.
Pair with a scoop of low-fat Greek yogurt for added protein and creaminess.

Almond Flour Brownies

 SERVES 12   **PREP TIME** 15 MIN.   **COOK TIME** 25 MIN.

Ingredients:
1 cup almond flour
1/4 cup unsweetened cocoa powder
1/2 teaspoon baking powder
1/4 teaspoon salt
2 large eggs
1/3 cup honey or maple syrup
1/4 cup unsweetened applesauce
1 teaspoon vanilla extract
1/4 cup dark chocolate chips
1/4 cup chopped walnuts

Nutritional Information
(Per Serving):

Calories: 110

Protein: 3g

Carbohydrates: 12g

Fats: 6g

Fiber: 2g

Cholesterol: 30mg

Sodium: 80mg

Potassium: 120mg

Directions:
Preheat your oven to 350°F (175°C). Line an 8x8-inch baking pan with parchment paper or lightly grease it with cooking spray.
Whisk together the almond flour, unsweetened cocoa powder, baking powder, and salt in a medium bowl.
Beat the eggs in a large bowl. Add the honey or maple syrup, unsweetened applesauce, and vanilla extract. Mix until well combined.
Gradually add the dry ingredients to the wet ingredients, stirring until combined. Do not overmix.Fold in the dark chocolate chips and chopped walnuts, if using.
Pour the batter into the prepared baking pan, spreading it evenly with a spatula.Bake in the preheated oven for 20-25 minutes, or until a toothpick inserted into the center comes out clean.Allow the brownies to cool completely in the pan before cutting them into squares.

Serving Suggestions:
Enjoy the brownies as a healthy dessert or snack.
Pair with a glass of almond milk or a cup of herbal tea for a delightful treat.

DESSERTS

Lemon & Violet Drizzle Cake

 SERVES 12   **PREP TIME** 20 MIN.   **COOK TIME** 40 MIN.

Ingredients:
Cake:
1 1/2 cups whole wheat flour
1/2 cup almond flour
1/2 teaspoon baking powder
1/2 teaspoon baking soda
1/4 teaspoon salt
3 large eggs
1/2 cup unsweetened applesauce
1/3 cup honey or maple syrup
1/4 cup unsweetened almond milk
1/4 cup fresh lemon juice
Zest of 1 lemon
1 teaspoon vanilla extract
Drizzle:
1/4 cup fresh lemon juice
2 tablespoons honey or maple syrup
1 tablespoon violet syrup

> **Nutritional Information (Per Serving):**
> Calories: 160
> Protein: 4g
> Carbohydrates: 24g
> Fats: 5g
> Fiber: 3g
> Cholesterol: 45mg
> Sodium: 110mg
> Potassium: 120mg

Directions:
Preheat your oven to 350°F (175°C). Grease and flour a 9x5-inch loaf pan or line it with parchment paper.
Whisk together the whole wheat flour, almond flour, baking powder, baking soda, and salt in a medium bowl.
Beat the eggs in a large bowl. Add the unsweetened applesauce, honey or maple syrup, unsweetened almond milk, fresh lemon juice, lemon zest, and vanilla extract. Mix until well combined. Gradually add the dry ingredients to the wet ingredients, stirring until combined. Do not overmix.
Pour the batter into the prepared loaf pan, spreading it evenly with a spatula. Bake in the preheated oven for 35-40 minutes, or until a toothpick inserted into the center comes out clean. Allow the cake to cool in the pan for 10 minutes, then transfer to a wire rack to cool completely. In a small bowl, whisk together the fresh lemon juice, honey or maple syrup, and violet syrup (if using) until well combined. Once the cake is completely cool, poke small holes on the top with a toothpick or skewer. Slowly pour the drizzle over the cake, allowing it to soak in. For best results, cover and refrigerate the cake for 30 minutes before serving to allow the flavors to meld and the drizzle to set.

Serving Suggestions:
Enjoy the Lemon & Violet Drizzle Cake as a delightful dessert or a special treat with afternoon tea.

Lemon and Blueberry Sorbet

 SERVES 4   **PREP TIME** 10 MIN.   **COOK TIME** 5 MIN.

Ingredients:
2 cups fresh or frozen blueberries
1/2 cup fresh lemon juice
1/4 cup honey or maple syrup
1 cup water
Zest of 1 lemon
Fresh mint leaves

> **Nutritional Information (Per Serving):**
> Calories: 80
> Protein: 0.5g
> Carbohydrates: 20g
> Fiber: 2g
> Sodium: 5mg
> Potassium: 60mg

Directions:
In a small saucepan, combine the water and honey or maple syrup. Heat over medium heat, stirring until the sweetener is fully dissolved. Remove from heat and let cool.
Combine the blueberries, fresh lemon juice, lemon zest, and the cooled simple syrup in a blender or food processor. Blend until smooth. For a smoother sorbet, strain the mixture through a fine mesh sieve to remove the blueberry skins and seeds. This step is optional and based on personal preference.
Pour the blended mixture into a shallow dish or a freezer-safe container. Cover and refrigerate for about 1 hour to chill.
After chilling, transfer the mixture to the freezer. Stir every 30 minutes for the first 2 hours to break up ice crystals and ensure a smooth texture. Let the sorbet freeze entirely for 2 hours or until firm. Scoop the sorbet into bowls or glasses. Garnish with fresh mint leaves if desired.

Serving Suggestions:
Serve the Lemon and Blueberry Sorbet as a refreshing dessert or a palate cleanser between courses.

DESSERTS

Apricot & Raspberry Tart

 SERVES 8   **PREP TIME** 20 MIN.   **COOK TIME** 30 MIN.

Ingredients:

Crust:
1 1/2 cups almond flour
1/4 cup coconut flour
1/4 cup honey or maple syrup
1/4 cup unsweetened applesauce
1/4 teaspoon salt
1 teaspoon vanilla extract

Filling:
1 cup fresh apricots, pitted and sliced
1 cup fresh raspberries
2 tablespoons honey or maple syrup
1 teaspoon lemon juice
1 tablespoon cornstarch

Topping:
1/4 cup sliced almonds

> **Nutritional Information (Per Serving):**
> Calories: 170
> Protein: 4g
> Carbohydrates: 22g
> Fats: 8g
> Fiber: 4g
> Sodium: 30mg
> Potassium: 200mg

Directions:

Preheat your oven to 350°F (175°C). Grease a 9-inch tart pan or pie dish with cooking spray.
Mix the almond flour, coconut flour, honey or maple syrup, unsweetened applesauce, salt, and vanilla extract in a medium bowl until a dough forms.
Press the dough evenly into the bottom and sides of the prepared tart pan.Bake in the oven for 10-12 minutes, or until the crust is lightly golden. Remove from the oven and let it cool slightly while preparing the filling.
Combine the sliced apricots, raspberries, honey or maple syrup, lemon juice, and cornstarch in a large bowl. Gently toss to coat the fruit evenly.Spread the fruit mixture evenly over the cooled crust.Return the tart to the oven and bake for an additional 20-25 minutes, or until the fruit is tender and bubbly.Remove the tart from the oven and let it cool to room temperature. For best results, chill in the refrigerator for 30 minutes before serving.If using sliced almonds, sprinkle them over the tart just before serving.

Serving Suggestions:

Serve the Apricot & Raspberry Tart as a delightful dessert or a special treat with afternoon tea.
Pair with a dollop of low-fat Greek yogurt or a scoop of sorbet for added creaminess and flavor.

Coconut Macaroons

 SERVES 12   **PREP TIME** 15 MIN.   **COOK TIME** 20 MIN.

Ingredients:

2 cups unsweetened shredded coconut
1/4 cup almond flour
1/4 cup honey or maple syrup
2 large egg whites
1 teaspoon vanilla extract
1/4 teaspoon salt
1/4 cup dark chocolate chips

> **Nutritional Information (Per Serving):**
> Calories: 80
> Protein: 1.5g
> Carbohydrates: 9g
> Fats: 5g
> Fiber: 2g
> Sodium: 30mg
> Potassium: 50mg

Directions:

Preheat your oven to 325°F (160°C). Line a baking sheet with parchment paper.
Mix the unsweetened shredded coconut and almond flour in a medium bowl.
Whisk the egg whites, honey or maple syrup, vanilla extract, and salt until frothy in a separate bowl.
Pour the wet mixture into the dry ingredients and stir until well combined.
Using a tablespoon or small ice cream scoop, place the mixture into small mounds onto the prepared baking sheet.
Bake in the preheated oven for 18-20 minutes or until the edges are golden brown.
Allow the macaroons to cool on the baking sheet for a few minutes, then transfer to a wire rack to cool completely.
If using dark chocolate, melt the chocolate chips in a microwave-safe bowl in 30-second intervals, stirring after each interval until smooth.Drizzle the melted chocolate over the cooled macaroons and let them set. For quicker setting, place the macaroons in the refrigerator for 15 minutes.

Serving Suggestions:

Enjoy the Coconut Macaroons as a healthy dessert or a sweet snack.
Pair with a cup of herbal tea or almond milk for a delightful treat.

DESSERTS

Healthy Apple Crunch

 SERVES 6 **PREP TIME** 15 MIN. **COOK TIME** 30 MIN.

Ingredients:
Filling:
4 medium apples
2 tablespoons lemon juice
1/4 cup honey or maple syrup
1 teaspoon ground cinnamon
1/4 teaspoon ground nutmeg
1/4 teaspoon ground ginger
Topping:
1 cup old-fashioned rolled oats
1/2 cup almond flour
1/4 cup chopped walnuts or pecans
1/4 cup honey or maple syrup
1/4 cup unsweetened applesauce
1 teaspoon vanilla extract
1/4 teaspoon salt

Nutritional Information (Per Serving):
Calories: 190
Protein: 3g
Carbohydrates: 34g
Fats: 5g
Fiber: 5g
Sodium: 50mg
Potassium: 200mg

Directions:
Preheat your oven to 350°F (175°C). Lightly grease an 8x8-inch baking dish or a similar-sized oven-safe dish.
In a large bowl, combine the sliced apples with lemon juice, honey or maple syrup, ground cinnamon, ground nutmeg, and ground ginger. Toss to coat the apples evenly.Spread the apple mixture evenly in the prepared baking dish.
In a medium bowl, mix the rolled oats, almond flour, chopped walnuts or pecans (if using), honey or maple syrup, unsweetened applesauce, vanilla extract, and salt until well combined.Sprinkle the oat mixture evenly over the apple filling.
Bake in the oven for 25-30 minutes or until the topping is golden brown and the apples are tender.

Serving Suggestions:
Serve the Healthy Apple Crunch warm as a dessert or a nutritious snack.
Pair with a dollop of low-fat Greek yogurt or a scoop of banana ice cream for added creaminess and flavor.

Matcha Green Tea Ice Cream

 SERVES 6 **PREP TIME** 15 MIN. **COOK TIME** 10 MIN.

Ingredients:
2 cups unsweetened almond milk
1 cup unsweetened coconut milk
1/4 cup honey or maple syrup
2 tablespoons matcha green tea powder
1 teaspoon vanilla extract
2 tablespoons cornstarch mixed
with 2 tablespoons water to form a slurry
Fresh mint leaves

Nutritional Information (Per Serving):
Calories: 90
Protein: 1.5g
Carbohydrates: 16g
Fats: 3g
Fiber: 1g
Sodium: 20mg
Potassium: 60mg

Directions:
Combine the unsweetened almond milk, unsweetened coconut milk, honey or maple syrup, matcha green tea powder, and vanilla extract in a medium saucepan.Whisk the mixture over medium heat until it is smooth, and the matcha is fully dissolved.
Once the mixture is hot but not boiling, add the cornstarch slurry.Continue to cook, stirring constantly, until the mixture thickens slightly (about 2-3 minutes).
Remove the saucepan from heat and allow the mixture to cool to room temperature.
Once the mixture has cooled, transfer it to a covered container and refrigerate for at least 4 hours or overnight.
After chilling, pour the mixture into an ice cream maker and churn according to the manufacturer's instructions until it reaches a soft-serve consistency.
Transfer the churned ice cream to a freezer-safe container.
Freeze for at least 2 hours or until firm.

Serving Suggestions:
Enjoy the Matcha Green Tea Ice Cream as a refreshing dessert or snack.
Pair with a sprinkle of toasted coconut flakes or a few fresh berries for added texture and flavor.

DESSERTS

Gooey Peanut Butter and Chocolate Fridge Bars

 SERVES 12 BARS   **PREP TIME** 15 MIN.   **COOK TIME** 5 MIN

Chilling Time: 2 hours

Ingredients:
1 cup rolled oats
1/2 cup natural peanut butter
(no added sugar or salt)
1/4 cup honey or maple syrup
1/4 cup unsweetened almond milk
1/4 cup ground flaxseed
2 tablespoons unsweetened
cocoa powder
1 teaspoon vanilla extract
1/4 teaspoon salt
1/4 cup dark chocolate chips
1/4 cup chopped nuts or seeds

Nutritional Information (Per Serving):
Calories: 140
Protein: 4g
Carbohydrates: 15g
Fats: 8g
Fiber: 3g
Sodium: 50mg
Potassium: 150mg

Directions:
In a large bowl, combine the rolled oats, natural peanut butter, honey or maple syrup, unsweetened almond milk, ground flaxseed, unsweetened cocoa powder, vanilla extract, and salt.Mix until well combined and a thick, sticky dough forms.
Fold in the dark chocolate chips and chopped nuts or seeds for added texture and flavor.
Line an 8x8-inch baking pan with parchment paper. Press the mixture evenly into the pan, smoothing the top with a spatula.
Cover the pan with plastic wrap or aluminum foil and refrigerate for at least 2 hours or until the mixture is firm.
Once chilled and firm, lift the mixture out of the pan using the parchment paper. Cut into 12 bars.
If desired, melt additional dark chocolate chips in a microwave-safe bowl in 30-second intervals, stirring until smooth.
Drizzle the melted chocolate over the bars and allow it to set.
Store the bars in an airtight container in the refrigerator for up to a week.

Serving Suggestions:
Enjoy the Gooey Peanut Butter and Chocolate Fridge Bars as a healthy snack or dessert.
Pair with a cup of herbal tea or almond milk for a nutritious treat.

Flourless Chocolate Cake

 SERVES 8   **PREP TIME** 15 MIN.   **COOK TIME** 25 MIN.

Ingredients:
1 cup dark chocolate chips
(at least 70% cocoa)
1/2 cup unsweetened applesauce
1/4 cup honey or maple syrup
3 large eggs
1/4 cup unsweetened cocoa powder
1 teaspoon vanilla extract
1/4 teaspoon salt
Fresh berries and mint leaves

Nutritional Information (Per Serving):
Calories: 150
Protein: 4g
Carbohydrates: 22g
Fats: 6g
Fiber: 3g
Cholesterol: 70mg
Sodium: 70mg
Potassium: 180mg

Directions:
Preheat your oven to 350°F (175°C). Grease an 8-inch round cake pan and line the bottom with parchment paper.
In a microwave-safe bowl, melt the dark chocolate chips in 30-second intervals, stirring after each interval until smooth. Allow to cool slightly.
Whisk together the unsweetened applesauce, honey or maple syrup, eggs, and vanilla extract in a large bowl until well combined.
Slowly pour the melted chocolate into the wet mixture, whisking continuously to prevent the eggs from curdling.
Sift in the unsweetened cocoa powder and add the salt.
Gently fold the mixture until well combined and smooth.
Pour the batter into the prepared cake pan and smooth the top with a spatula.Bake in the preheated oven for 20-25 minutes, or until a toothpick inserted into the center comes out clean.
Allow the cake to cool in the pan for 10 minutes, then transfer to a wire rack to cool completely. For best results, chill in the refrigerator for at least 1 hour before serving.
Garnish with fresh berries and mint leaves if desired.Slice and serve.

Serving Suggestions:
Enjoy the Flourless Chocolate Cake as a decadent dessert or a special treat.
Pair with a dollop of low-fat Greek yogurt or a scoop of berry sorbet for added flavor and creaminess.

DESSERTS

Strawberry and Basil Sorbet

 SERVES 4 **PREP TIME** 15 MIN. **COOK TIME** 20 MIN.

Ingredients:
4 cups fresh strawberries
1/4 cup honey or maple syrup
1/4 cup fresh basil leaves
2 tablespoons fresh lemon juice
1/2 cup water

Nutritional Information (Per Serving):

Calories: 80

Protein: 1g

Carbohydrates: 20g

Fiber: 2g

Potassium: 180mgg

Directions:
Wash, hull, and halve the strawberries.

Combine the strawberries, honey or maple syrup, fresh basil leaves, lemon juice, and water in a blender or food processor. Blend until smooth.

Strain the mixture through a fine mesh sieve to remove seeds and basil bits for a smoother texture. This step is optional and based on personal preference.

Pour the blended mixture into a covered container and refrigerate for at least 1 hour to chill.

After chilling, transfer the mixture to an ice cream maker and churn according to the manufacturer's instructions until it reaches a soft-serve consistency.

Transfer the churned sorbet to a freezer-safe container. Freeze for at least 3 hours or until firm.

Serving Suggestions:
Enjoy the Strawberry and Basil Sorbet as a refreshing dessert or snack.

Coconut and Lime Panna Cotta

 SERVES 4 **PREP TIME** 15 MIN. **COOK TIME** 10 MIN.

Ingredients:
1 cup unsweetened coconut milk
1 cup unsweetened almond milk
1/4 cup honey or maple syrup
2 tablespoons fresh lime juice
1 teaspoon lime zest
1 teaspoon vanilla extract
1 packet unflavored gelatin
3 tablespoons water

Nutritional Information (Per Serving):

Calories: 130

Protein: 3g

Carbohydrates: 15g

Fats: 6g

Fiber: 1g

Sodium: 30mg

Potassium: 130mg

Directions:
In a small bowl, sprinkle the gelatin over three tablespoons of water and let it bloom for about 5 minutes.

Combine the unsweetened coconut milk, unsweetened almond milk, honey or maple syrup, fresh lime juice, lime zest, and vanilla extract in a medium saucepan.Heat the mixture over medium heat, stirring occasionally, until it is hot but not boiling.

Remove the saucepan from heat and add the bloomed gelatin to the hot milk mixture.Stir well until the gelatin is completely dissolved.

Strain the mixture through a fine mesh sieve into a large measuring cup or bowl to remove any undissolved gelatin or lime zest bits.

Pour the mixture into 4 ramekins or dessert glasses.

Refrigerate for at least 4 hours or until set.

Serving Suggestions:
Serve the Coconut and Lime Panna Cotta as a light and refreshing dessert.

DESSERTS

Chocolate Dipped Strawberries

 SERVES 4   **PREP TIME** 15 MIN.   **COOK TIME** 30 MIN.

Ingredients:
16 large fresh strawberries
1/2 cup dark chocolate chips
(at least 70% cocoa)
1 teaspoon coconut oil
1 tablespoon chopped nuts
or shredded coconut

Nutritional Information (Per Serving):

Calories: 90

Protein: 1g

Carbohydrates: 13g

Fats: 5g

Fiber: 3g

Potassium: 190 mg

Directions:
Wash the strawberries and pat them dry thoroughly with a paper towel. Ensure they are completely dry to prevent the chocolate from seizing.

In a microwave-safe bowl, combine the dark chocolate chips and coconut oil (if using).Microwave in 30-second intervals, stirring after each interval until the chocolate is completely melted and smooth.

Hold each strawberry by the stem and dip it into the melted chocolate, ensuring it is evenly coated.Allow excess chocolate to drip off before placing the strawberry on a parchment-lined baking sheet.

If desired, sprinkle chopped nuts or shredded coconut over the chocolate-coated strawberries before the chocolate sets.

Place the baking sheet in the refrigerator for at least 30 minutes to allow the chocolate to set completely.

Serving Suggestions:
Enjoy the Chocolate Dipped Strawberries as a healthy dessert or a sweet snack.

Baked Pears with Honey and Walnuts

SERVES 4   **PREP TIME** 10 MIN.   **COOK TIME** 25 MIN.

Ingredients:
2 large pears
2 tablespoons honey
1/4 cup chopped walnuts
1 teaspoon ground cinnamon
1/4 teaspoon ground nutmeg
1 teaspoon vanilla extract
1 tablespoon fresh lemon juice
1/4 cup water

Nutritional Information (Per Serving):

Calories: 130

Protein: 1g

Carbohydrates: 22g

Fats: 5g

Fiber: 4g

Potassium: 150mg

Directions:
Preheat your oven to 350°F (175°C).

Wash the pears, cut them in half, and core them using a melon baller or a small spoon.Place the pear halves in a baking dish, cut side up.

In a small bowl, mix the honey, chopped walnuts, ground cinnamon, ground nutmeg, and vanilla extract until well combined.

Spoon the honey-walnut mixture into the cored centers of each pear half.

Drizzle the fresh lemon juice over the pears.Pour the water into the bottom of the baking dish to help steam the pears as they bake.

Cover the baking dish with aluminum foil and bake in the oven for 20 minutes.Remove the foil and bake for 5 minutes, or until the pears are tender and the topping is golden brown.

Serving Suggestions:
Enjoy the Baked Pears with Honey and Walnuts as a healthy dessert or a sweet snack.

Pair with a dollop of low-fat Greek yogurt or a scoop of vanilla almond milk ice cream for added creaminess and flavor.

SMOOTHIES

Plum and Green Tea Metabolism Smoothie

 SERVES 2   **PREP TIME** 10 MIN.   **COOK TIME** 30 MIN.

Ingredients:
2 medium plums
1 cup brewed green tea
1/2 cup unsweetened almond milk
1 tablespoon honey or maple syrup
1 tablespoon chia seeds
1/2 teaspoon ground ginger
1 cup ice cubes
Fresh mint leaves

Nutritional Information (Per Serving):

Calories: 90

Protein: 2g

Carbohydrates: 17g

Fats: 2g

Fiber: 4g

Sodium: 30mg

Potassium: 180mg

Directions:
Brew the green tea and allow it to cool. This can be done beforehand, and the tea can be chilled in the refrigerator.Pit and chop the plums.

In a blender, combine the chopped plums, cooled green tea, unsweetened almond milk, honey or maple syrup (if using), chia seeds, ground ginger, and ice cubes.Blend until smooth and creamy.

If the smoothie is too thick, add a little more almond milk or green tea until it reaches the desired consistency.

Chill in the refrigerator for 30 minutes before serving for a colder smoothie.

Serving Suggestions:
Enjoy the Plum and Green Tea Metabolism Smoothie as a refreshing breakfast or a revitalizing snack.

Grapefruit and Honey Immune Boost Smoothie

 SERVES 2   **PREP TIME** 10 MIN.   **COOK TIME** 30 MIN.

Ingredients:
1 large grapefruit
1 medium orange
1/2 cup unsweetened almond milk
1 tablespoon honey
1 tablespoon chia seeds
1 teaspoon grated fresh ginger
1/2 teaspoon turmeric powder
1/2 cup ice cubes
Fresh mint leaves

Nutritional Information (Per Serving):

Calories: 110

Protein: 2g

Carbohydrates: 25g

Fats: 1g

Fiber: 4g

Sodium: 30mg

Potassium: 250mg

Directions:
Peel and segment the grapefruit and orange, removing any seeds.Grate the fresh ginger.

In a blender, combine the grapefruit segments, orange segments, unsweetened almond milk, honey, chia seeds, grated ginger, turmeric powder, and ice cubes.Blend until smooth and creamy.

If the smoothie is too thick, add more almond milk until the desired consistency is reached.

Chill in the refrigerator for 30 minutes before serving for a colder smoothie.

Serving Suggestions:
Enjoy the Grapefruit and Honey Immune Boost Smoothie as a refreshing breakfast or a revitalizing snack.

SMOOTHIES

Watermelon and Basil Refreshing Smoothie

 SERVES 2   **PREP TIME** 10 MIN.   **COOK TIME** 30 MIN.

Ingredients:
3 cups seedless watermelon
1/2 cup unsweetened coconut water
1 tablespoon fresh lime juice
6-8 fresh basil leaves
1 tablespoon chia seeds
1/2 cup ice cubes
Honey or maple syrup to taste

Nutritional Information (Per Serving):
Calories: 70
Protein: 1g
Carbohydrates: 17g
Fats: 0.5g
Fiber: 2g
Sodium: 20mg
Potassium: 180mg

Directions:
Cube the seedless watermelon. Juice the lime.
Combine the watermelon cubes, unsweetened coconut water, fresh lime juice, basil leaves, chia seeds, and ice cubes in a blender. Blend until smooth and well combined.
Taste the smoothie and add honey or maple syrup if you desire additional sweetness. Blend again briefly to combine.
Chill in the refrigerator for 30 minutes before serving for a colder and more refreshing smoothie.

Serving Suggestions:
Enjoy the Watermelon and Basil Refreshing Smoothie as a cooling snack or a hydrating post-workout drink.

Berry and Spinach Detox Smoothie

 SERVES 2   **PREP TIME** 10 MIN. **COOK TIME** 10 MIN.

Ingredients:
1 cup fresh or frozen mixed berries
1 cup fresh spinach leaves
1/2 cup unsweetened almond milk
1/2 cup plain Greek yogurt
1 tablespoon chia seeds
1 tablespoon fresh lemon juice
1/2 teaspoon grated fresh ginger
1/2 cup ice cubes
Honey or maple syrup to taste

Nutritional Information (Per Serving):
Calories: 110
Protein: 6g
Carbohydrates: 18g
Fats: 2g
Fiber: 5g
Cholesterol: 5mg
Sodium: 60mg
Potassium: 300mg

Directions:
Wash the berries and spinach leaves. Grate the fresh ginger.
Combine the mixed berries, fresh spinach leaves, unsweetened almond milk, plain Greek yogurt, chia seeds, fresh lemon juice, grated ginger, and ice cubes in a blender. Blend until smooth and well combined.
Taste the smoothie and add honey or maple syrup if you desire additional sweetness. Blend again briefly to combine.
Chill in the refrigerator for 10 minutes before serving for a colder and more refreshing smoothie.

Serving Suggestions:
Enjoy the Berry and Spinach Detox Smoothie as a refreshing breakfast or a revitalizing snack.
Pair with a handful of nuts or whole fruit for added nutrition.

SMOOTHIES

Mango and Turmeric Anti-Inflammatory Smoothie

 SERVES 2 **PREP TIME** 10 MIN. **COOK TIME** 10 MIN.

Ingredients:

1 cup fresh or frozen mango chunks
1/2 cup unsweetened almond milk
1/2 cup plain Greek yogurt
1 teaspoon turmeric powder
1/2 teaspoon grated fresh ginger
1 tablespoon chia seeds
1 tablespoon honey or maple syrup
1/2 cup ice cubes
Fresh mint leaves

Nutritional Information (Per Serving):

Calories: 130

Protein: 5g

Carbohydrates: 24g

Fats: 2g

Fiber: 4g

Cholesterol: 5mg

Sodium: 50mg

Potassium: 300mg

Directions:

If fresh mango is used, peel and chop it into chunks.Grate the fresh ginger.

Combine the mango chunks, unsweetened almond milk, plain Greek yogurt, turmeric powder, grated ginger, chia seeds, honey or maple syrup (if using), and ice cubes.Blend until smooth and creamy.

Taste the smoothie and add more honey or maple syrup if desired. Blend again briefly to mix.

Chill in the refrigerator for 10 minutes before serving for a colder and more refreshing smoothie.

Serving Suggestions:

Enjoy the Mango and Turmeric Anti-Inflammatory Smoothie as a refreshing breakfast or a revitalizing snack.

Green Goddess Smoothie with Kale & Avocado

 SERVES 2 **PREP TIME** 10 MIN. **COOK TIME** 10 MIN.

Ingredients:

1 cup fresh kale leaves
1/2 ripe avocado
1 medium banana
1/2 cup unsweetened almond milk
1/2 cup plain Greek yogurt
1/2 cup water
1 tablespoon chia seeds
1 tablespoon fresh lemon juice
1/2 teaspoon grated fresh ginger
1/2 cup ice cubes
Honey or maple syrup to taste

Nutritional Information (Per Serving):

Calories: 170

Protein: 6g

Carbohydrates: 25g

Fats: 7g

Fiber: 6g

Cholesterol: 5mg

Sodium: 70mg

Potassium: 500mg

Directions:

Wash the kale leaves and remove the stems.Scoop out the flesh of the avocado.Peel the banana.Grate the fresh ginger.

Combine the kale leaves, avocado, banana, unsweetened almond milk, plain Greek yogurt, water, chia seeds, fresh lemon juice, grated ginger, and ice cubes in a blender.Blend until smooth and creamy.

Taste the smoothie and add honey or maple syrup if you desire additional sweetness. Blend again briefly to combine.

Chill in the refrigerator for 10 minutes before serving for a colder and more refreshing smoothie.

Serving Suggestions:

Enjoy the Green Goddess Smoothie as a refreshing breakfast or a revitalizing snack.

SMOOTHIES

Pear and Ginger Detox Smoothie

 SERVES 2   **PREP TIME** 10 MIN.   **COOK TIME** 10 MIN.

Ingredients:

2 ripe pears
1 cup spinach leaves
1/2 cup unsweetened almond milk
1/2 cup plain Greek yogurt
1 tablespoon chia seeds
1 tablespoon fresh lemon juice
1 teaspoon grated fresh ginger
1/2 cup ice cubes
Honey or maple syrup to taste

Nutritional Information (Per Serving):

Calories: 140

Protein: 5g

Carbohydrates: 26g

Fats: 2g

Fiber: 5g

Cholesterol: 5mg

Sodium: 50mg

Potassium: 350mg

Directions:

Wash and chop the pears, removing the cores. Wash the spinach leaves. Grate the fresh ginger.

Combine the chopped pears, spinach leaves, unsweetened almond milk, plain Greek yogurt, chia seeds, fresh lemon juice, grated ginger, and ice cubes in a blender. Blend until smooth and creamy.

Taste the smoothie and add honey or maple syrup if you desire additional sweetness. Blend again briefly to combine. Chill in the refrigerator for 10 minutes before serving for a colder and more refreshing smoothie.

Serving Suggestions:

Enjoy the Pear and Ginger Detox Smoothie as a refreshing breakfast or a revitalizing snack.

Cherry & Almond Antioxidant Smoothie

 SERVES 2   **PREP TIME** 10 MIN. **COOK TIME** 10 MIN.

Ingredients:

1 cup fresh or frozen cherries
1/2 banana
1/2 cup unsweetened almond milk
1/2 cup plain Greek yogurt
1 tablespoon almond butter
1 tablespoon chia seeds
1 teaspoon almond extract
1/2 cup ice cubes
Honey or maple syrup to taste

Nutritional Information (Per Serving):

Calories: 180

Protein: 7g

Carbohydrates: 25g

Fats: 6g

Fiber: 5g

Cholesterol: 5mg

Sodium: 70mg

Potassium: 400mg

Directions:

Pit the cherries if using fresh. Peel and slice the banana. Combine the cherries, banana, unsweetened almond milk, plain Greek yogurt, almond butter, chia seeds, almond extract, and ice cubes in a blender. Blend until smooth and creamy. Taste the smoothie and add honey or maple syrup if you desire additional sweetness. Blend again briefly to combine. Chill in the refrigerator for 10 minutes before serving for a colder and more refreshing smoothie.

Serving Suggestions:

Enjoy the Cherry & Almond Antioxidant Smoothie as a refreshing breakfast or a revitalizing snack.

SMOOTHIES

Beet and Berry Liver Cleanse Smoothie

 SERVES 2   **PREP TIME** 10 MIN.   **COOK TIME** 10 MIN.

Ingredients:
1 small beet
1 cup mixed berries
1/2 banana
1 cup unsweetened almond milk
1/2 cup plain Greek yogurt
1 tablespoon chia seeds
1 tablespoon fresh lemon juice
1/2 cup ice cubes
Honey or maple syrup to taste

Nutritional Information (Per Serving):

Calories: 140

Protein: 6g

Carbohydrates: 27g

Fats: 2g

Fiber: 5g

Cholesterol: 5mg

Sodium: 70mg

Potassium: 450mg

Directions:
Peel and chop the beet into small pieces.Peel and slice the banana.Wash the mixed berries.

Combine the chopped beet, mixed berries, banana, unsweetened almond milk, plain Greek yogurt, chia seeds, fresh lemon juice, and ice cubes in a blender.Blend until smooth and creamy.

Taste the smoothie and add honey or maple syrup if you desire additional sweetness. Blend again briefly to combine. Chill in the refrigerator for 10 minutes before serving for a colder and more refreshing smoothie.

Serving Suggestions:
Enjoy the Beet and Berry Liver Cleanse Smoothie as a refreshing breakfast or a revitalizing snack.

Carrot and Orange Vitamin C Smoothie

 SERVES 2   **PREP TIME** 10 MIN.   **COOK TIME** 10 MIN.

Ingredients:
2 medium carrots
1 large orange
1/2 banana
1 cup unsweetened almond milk
1/2 cup plain Greek yogurt
1 tablespoon chia seeds
1 tablespoon fresh lemon juice
1/2 teaspoon grated fresh ginger
1/2 cup ice cubes
Honey or maple syrup to taste

Nutritional Information (Per Serving):

Calories: 160

Protein: 7g

Carbohydrates: 29g

Fats: 2g

Fiber: 5g

Cholesterol: 5mg

Sodium: 60mg

Potassium: 500mg

Directions:
Peel and chop the carrots.Peel and segment the orange.Peel and slice the banana.Grate the fresh ginger.

Combine the chopped carrots, orange segments, banana, unsweetened almond milk, plain Greek yogurt, chia seeds, fresh lemon juice, grated ginger, and ice cubes in a blender. Blend until smooth and creamy.

Taste the smoothie and add honey or maple syrup if you desire additional sweetness. Blend again briefly to combine. Chill in the refrigerator for 10 minutes before serving for a colder and more refreshing smoothie.

Serving Suggestions:
Enjoy the Carrot and Orange Vitamin C Smoothie as a refreshing breakfast or a revitalizing snack.

SMOOTHIES

Banana and Flax Seed Omega-3 Smoothie

 SERVES 2   **PREP TIME** 10 MIN.   **COOK TIME** 10 MIN.

Ingredients:
2 medium bananas
1 cup unsweetened almond milk
1/2 cup plain Greek yogurt
2 tablespoons ground flax seeds
1 tablespoon chia seeds
1 tablespoon honey or maple syrup
1/2 teaspoon vanilla extract
1/2 cup ice cubes
Fresh mint leaves

Nutritional Information (Per Serving):

Calories: 220

Protein: 8g

Carbohydrates: 33g

Fats: 7g

Fiber: 8g

Cholesterol: 5mg

Sodium: 60mg

Potassium: 600mg

Directions:
Peel the bananas.
Combine the bananas, unsweetened almond milk, plain Greek yogurt, ground flax seeds, chia seeds, honey or maple syrup (if using), vanilla extract, and ice cubes.Blend until smooth and creamy.
Taste the smoothie and add more honey or maple syrup if you desire additional sweetness. Blend again briefly to combine.
Chill in the refrigerator for 10 minutes before serving for a colder and more refreshing smoothie.

Serving Suggestions:
Enjoy the Banana and Flax Seed Omega-3 Smoothie as a nutritious breakfast or a revitalizing snack.

Papaya and Lime Enzyme-Rich Smoothie

 SERVES 2   **PREP TIME** 10 MIN.   **COOK TIME** 10 MIN.

Ingredients:
2 cups ripe papaya
1 cup unsweetened coconut water
1/2 cup plain Greek yogurt
1 tablespoon fresh lime juice
1 teaspoon lime zest
1 tablespoon chia seeds
1 tablespoon honey or maple syrup
1/2 cup ice cubes
Fresh mint leaves

Nutritional Information (Per Serving):

Calories: 130

Protein: 5g

Carbohydrates: 23g

Fats: 2g

Fiber: 4g

Cholesterol: 5mg

Sodium: 50mg

Potassium: 350mg

Directions:
Peel, seed, and cube the ripe papaya.Zest and juice the lime.
Combine the papaya cubes, unsweetened coconut water, plain Greek yogurt, fresh lime juice, lime zest, chia seeds, honey or maple syrup (if using), and ice cubes.Blend until smooth and creamy.
Taste the smoothie and add more honey or maple syrup if you desire additional sweetness. Blend again briefly to combine.
Chill in the refrigerator for 10 minutes before serving for a colder and more refreshing smoothie.

Serving Suggestions:
Enjoy the Papaya and Lime Enzyme-Rich Smoothie as a refreshing breakfast or a revitalizing snack.

SMOOTHIES

Kiwi and Coconut Water Electrolyte Smoothie

 SERVES 2   **PREP TIME** 10 MIN.   **COOK TIME** 20 MIN.

Ingredients:
2 ripe kiwi
1 cup unsweetened coconut water
1/2 cup fresh spinach leaves
1/2 cup cucumber
1/2 cup frozen pineapple chunks
1 tablespoon fresh lime juice
1 teaspoon chia seeds
1 teaspoon honey or stevia
Ice cubes

> **Nutritional Information (Per Serving):**
> Calories: 105
> Protein: 2g
> Carbohydrates: 25g
> Fats: 1g
> Fiber: 5g
> Sodium: 55mg
> Potassium: 470mg

Directions:
Wash and peel the kiwis, cucumber, and spinach. Chop them into small pieces for easy blending.

In a blender, combine the chopped kiwis, coconut water, spinach leaves, cucumber, frozen pineapple chunks, and lime juice. Blend until smooth.

Once the mixture is smooth, add the chia seeds and blend for a few more seconds to incorporate them.

If you prefer a sweeter smoothie, add honey or stevia to taste and blend again.

For a more refreshing drink, add ice cubes directly to the blender or chill the smoothie in the refrigerator for 20 minutes before serving.

Serving Suggestions:
Serve the smoothie as a refreshing breakfast option or a midday snack.

Peach and Spinach Iron-Rich Smoothie

 SERVES 2   **PREP TIME** 10 MIN.   **COOK TIME** 20 MIN.

Ingredients:
2 ripe peaches, pitted and chopped
1 cup fresh spinach leaves
1/2 cup unsweetened almond milk
1/2 cup plain Greek yogurt (low-fat)
1/4 cup rolled oats
1 tablespoon flax seeds
1 teaspoon fresh lemon juice
1 teaspoon honey or stevia
Ice cubes

> **Nutritional Information (Per Serving):**
> Calories: 190
> Protein: 7g
> Carbohydrates: 32g
> Fats: 4g
> Fiber: 6g
> Sodium: 95mg
> Potassium: 530mg
> Iron: 2.5mg

Directions:
Wash the peaches and spinach. Pitch the peaches into small pieces, leaving the skin on for added fiber.

In a blender, combine the chopped peaches, fresh spinach leaves, almond milk, Greek yogurt, rolled oats, flaxseeds, and lemon juice. Blend until smooth.

If you prefer a sweeter smoothie, add honey or stevia to taste and blend again.

For a more refreshing drink, add ice cubes directly to the blender or chill the smoothie in the refrigerator for 20 minutes before serving.

Serving Suggestions:
Serve the smoothie as a nutritious breakfast option or a midday snack.

SMOOTHIES

Strawberry and Almond Butter Protein Smoothie

 SERVES 2   **PREP TIME** 10 MIN.   **COOK TIME** 20 MIN.

Ingredients:
1 cup fresh strawberries
1 medium banana, frozen
1 cup unsweetened almond milk
2 tablespoons almond butter
1 scoop vanilla protein powder
1 tablespoon chia seeds
1 teaspoon honey or stevia
Ice cubes

Nutritional Information (Per Serving):

Calories: 230

Protein: 15g

Carbohydrates: 25g

Fats: 10g

Fiber: 6g

Sodium: 180mg

Potassium: 450mg

Directions:
Start by washing and hulling the strawberries. Chop them into small pieces.
In a blender, combine the chopped strawberries, frozen banana, almond milk, almond butter, protein powder, and chia seeds. Blend until smooth.
If you prefer a sweeter smoothie, add honey or stevia to taste and blend again.
For a more refreshing drink, add ice cubes directly to the blender or chill the smoothie in the refrigerator for 20 minutes before serving.

Serving Suggestions:
Serve the smoothie as a nutritious breakfast option or a post-workout snack.

Cucumber and Mint Hydration Smoothie

 SERVES 2   **PREP TIME** 10 MIN. **COOK TIME** 20 MIN.

Ingredients:
1 large cucumber
1/2 cup fresh mint leaves
1 cup unsweetened coconut water
1/2 cup spinach leaves
1/2 green apple
1 tablespoon fresh lime juice
1 teaspoon chia seeds
1 teaspoon honey or stevia
Ice cubes

Nutritional Information (Per Serving):

Calories: 80

Protein: 2g

Carbohydrates: 18g

Fats: 1g

Fiber: 4g

Sodium: 50mg

Potassium: 450mg

Directions:
Wash and peel the cucumber and green apple, then chop them into small pieces. Wash the mint leaves and spinach.
In a blender, combine the chopped cucumber, mint leaves, coconut water, spinach leaves, green apple, and lime juice. Blend until smooth.
Once the mixture is smooth, add the chia seeds and blend for a few more seconds to incorporate them.
If you prefer a sweeter smoothie, add honey or stevia to taste and blend again.
For a more refreshing drink, add ice cubes directly to the blender or chill the smoothie in the refrigerator for 20 minutes before serving.

Serving Suggestions:
Serve the smoothie as a refreshing hydration option at any time of the day.

SMOOTHIES

Apple and Cinnamon Metabolism Boosting Smoothie

 SERVES 2   **PREP TIME** 10 MIN.   **COOK TIME** 20 MIN.

Ingredients:
2 medium apples
1 cup unsweetened almond milk
1/2 cup plain Greek yogurt (low-fat)
1/4 cup rolled oats
1 tablespoon ground flaxseed
1 teaspoon ground cinnamon
1 teaspoon fresh lemon juice
1 teaspoon honey or stevia
Ice cubes

Nutritional Information (Per Serving):

Calories: 210

Protein: 7g

Carbohydrates: 35g

Fats: 5g

Fiber: 6g

Sodium: 90mg

Potassium: 390mg

Directions:
Wash the apples thoroughly. Core and chop them into small pieces, leaving the skin on for added fiber.

In a blender, combine the chopped apples, almond milk, Greek yogurt, rolled oats, ground flaxseed, ground cinnamon, and lemon juice. Blend until smooth.

If you prefer a sweeter smoothie, add honey or stevia to taste and blend again.

For a more refreshing drink, add ice cubes directly to the blender or chill the smoothie in the refrigerator for 20 minutes before serving.

Serving Suggestions:
Serve the smoothie as a nutritious breakfast option or a midday snack.

Blueberry and Chia Seed Power Smoothie

 SERVES 2   **PREP TIME** 10 MIN.   **COOK TIME** 20 MIN.

Ingredients:
1 cup fresh or frozen blueberries
1 medium banana
1 cup unsweetened almond milk
1/2 cup plain Greek yogurt (low-fat)
1 tablespoon chia seeds
1 tablespoon ground flaxseed
1 teaspoon fresh lemon juice
1 teaspoon honey or stevia
Ice cubes

Nutritional Information (Per Serving):

Calories: 190

Protein: 8g

Carbohydrates: 30g

Fats: 5g

Fiber: 7g

Sodium: 80mg

Potassium: 420mg

Directions:
If using fresh blueberries, wash them thoroughly. Peel and freeze the banana ahead of time for a creamier texture.

In a blender, combine the blueberries, frozen banana, almond milk, Greek yogurt, chia seeds, ground flaxseed, and lemon juice. Blend until smooth.

If you prefer a sweeter smoothie, add honey or stevia to taste and blend again.

For a more refreshing drink, add ice cubes directly to the blender or chill the smoothie in the refrigerator for 20 minutes before serving.

Serving Suggestions:
Serve the smoothie as a nutritious breakfast option or a midday snack.

SMOOTHIES

Pineapple and Ginger Digestive Smoothie

 SERVES 2   **PREP TIME** 10 MIN.   **COOK TIME** 20 MIN.

Ingredients:
1 cup fresh or frozen pineapple chunks
1 medium banana
1 cup unsweetened coconut water
1/2 cup plain Greek yogurt (low-fat)
1 tablespoon fresh ginger
1 tablespoon chia seeds
1 teaspoon fresh lemon juice
1 teaspoon honey or stevia
Ice cubes

Nutritional Information (Per Serving):

Calories: 160

Protein: 6g

Carbohydrates: 30g

Fats: 2g

Fiber: 4g

Cholesterol: 0mg

Sodium: 60mg

Potassium: 450mg

Directions:
If fresh pineapple is used, peel and chop it into chunks. Peel and freeze the banana ahead of time for a creamier texture. Grate the fresh ginger.

In a blender, combine the pineapple chunks, frozen banana, coconut water, Greek yogurt, grated ginger, chia seeds, and lemon juice. Blend until smooth.

If you prefer a sweeter smoothie, add honey or stevia to taste and blend again.

For a more refreshing drink, add ice cubes directly to the blender or chill the smoothie in the refrigerator for 20 minutes before serving.

Serving Suggestions:
Serve the smoothie as a nutritious breakfast option or a midday snack.

Immune Boosting Smoothie

 SERVES 2   **PREP TIME** 10 MIN. **COOK TIME** 20 MIN.

Ingredients:
1 cup fresh or frozen mixed berries
1 medium orange, peeled and segmented
1/2 cup fresh spinach leaves
1/2 cup unsweetened almond milk
1/2 cup plain Greek yogurt (low-fat)
1 tablespoon ground flaxseed
1 teaspoon fresh lemon juice
1 teaspoon honey or stevia
1/2 teaspoon turmeric powder
Ice cubes

Nutritional Information (Per Serving):

Calories: 210

Protein: 7g

Carbohydrates: 35g

Fats: 5g

Fiber: 6g

Sodium: 90mg

Potassium: 390mg

Directions:
Wash the mixed berries and spinach leaves thoroughly. Peel and segment the orange.

In a blender, combine the mixed berries, orange segments, spinach leaves, almond milk, Greek yogurt, ground flaxseed, lemon juice, and turmeric powder. Blend until smooth.

If you prefer a sweeter smoothie, add honey or stevia to taste and blend again.

For a more refreshing drink, add ice cubes directly to the blender or chill the smoothie in the refrigerator for 20 minutes before serving.

Serving Suggestions:
Serve the smoothie as a nutritious breakfast option or a midday snack.

Beverages for Liver - Cleansing

Detoxifying Green Tea with Lemon

 SERVES 2   **PREP TIME** 5 MIN.   **COOK TIME** 5 MIN.

Ingredients:
2 cups water
2 green tea bags
1 medium lemon, juiced
1 teaspoon honey or stevia
Fresh mint leaves
Ice cubes

Nutritional Information (Per Serving):
Calories: 5
Carbohydrates: 1g
Potassium: 30mg

Directions:
Bring 2 cups of water to a boil in a saucepan or kettle.
Remove the water from the heat and add the green tea bags or loose-leaf green tea. Let it steep for 3-5 minutes, depending on your desired strength.
Remove the tea bags or strain the loose-leaf tea. Add the fresh lemon juice to the brewed tea.
If you prefer a sweeter tea, add honey or stevia to taste and stir well.
For a refreshing iced tea, let the tea cool to room temperature, then refrigerate for at least 20 minutes. Serve over ice cubes.

Serving Suggestions:
Serve the tea warm or chilled as a refreshing beverage at any time of the day. It pairs well with light snacks or meals focused on liver health.

Ginger and Turmeric Tea

 **SERVES** 4   **PREP TIME** 5 MIN.   **COOK TIME** 10 MIN.

Ingredients:
4 cups water
1-inch piece of fresh ginger
1-inch piece of fresh turmeric
1 teaspoon ground cinnamon
1 tablespoon fresh lemon juice
1 tablespoon honey or stevia
1 pinch black pepper
Fresh mint leaves

Nutritional Information (Per Serving):
Calories: 10
Protein: 0.2g
Carbohydrates: 2.5g
Fats: 0.1g
Fiber: 0.5g
Sodium: 5mg
Potassium: 30mg

Directions:
Bring the 4 cups of water to a boil in a medium-sized pot.
Once boiling, reduce the heat to low and add the ginger, turmeric, and cinnamon.
Let the mixture simmer gently for about 10-15 minutes. This allows the flavors to infuse and the beneficial compounds to be extracted into the water.
After simmering, strain the tea into a teapot or directly into cups, discarding the solids.
Add fresh lemon juice and honey or stevia for additional flavor and sweetness if desired. Stir well.
Add a pinch of black pepper to each cup to enhance the absorption of turmeric's curcumin.

Serving Suggestions:
Pair with a high-fiber, low-fat snack like a small handful of nuts or fruit.

Beverages for Liver - Cleansing

Coconut Water with Lime

 SERVES 4   **PREP TIME** 5 MIN.   **COOK TIME** 5 MIN.

Ingredients:
4 cups fresh coconut water
2 medium limes
1 tablespoon fresh mint leaves
1 teaspoon chia seeds
Ice cubes
Lime slices
Fresh mint sprigs

Nutritional Information (Per Serving):

Calories: 45

Protein: 0.5g

Carbohydrates: 11g

Sugars: 7g

Fats: 0.5g

Fiber: 2g

Sodium: 60mg

Potassium: 400mg

Directions:
Ensure all ingredients are ready. Juice the limes to get approximately 4 tablespoons of fresh lime juice.
Mix Ingredients: Combine coconut water and lime juice in a large pitcher. Stir well to mix.
Add the finely chopped mint leaves and chia seeds. Stir again to distribute evenly.
Place the pitcher in the refrigerator to chill for at least 30 minutes. This allows the flavors to meld together.

Serving Suggestions:
Serve this refreshing drink cold, ideally as a mid-morning or afternoon beverage.
Pair with a small snack, such as a handful of almonds or a piece of fresh fruit, for a balanced and liver-friendly treat.

Cucumber and Mint Infused Water

 SERVES 4   **PREP TIME** 5 MIN.   **COOK TIME** 5 MIN.

Ingredients:
1 medium cucumber
1/4 cup fresh mint leaves
8 cups water
1 lemon
Ice cubes

Nutritional Information (Per Serving):

Calories: 5

Protein: 0.1g

Carbohydrates: 1g

Fiber: 0.1g

Cholesterol: 0mg

Sodium: 2mg

Potassium: 40mg

Directions:
Wash the cucumber, mint leaves, and lemon thoroughly. Thinly slice the cucumber and lemon.
Add the sliced cucumber, mint leaves, and lemon slices (if using) to a large pitcher.
Pour 8 cups of water over the ingredients into the pitcher.
Place the pitcher in the refrigerator and let it chill for 1-2 hours to allow the flavors to infuse.
Before serving, stir the water well. If desired, fill glasses with ice cubes and pour the infused water over the ice.
Garnish with additional cucumber slices or mint leaves if desired.

Serving Suggestions:
Serve this refreshing infused water cold, ideally as a hydrating beverage throughout the day.
Pair with a light snack, such as a piece of fruit or a small handful of nuts, for a balanced and liver-friendly treat.

Beverages for Liver - Cleansing

Apple Cider Vinegar Tonic

 SERVES 4   **PREP TIME 5 MIN.**   **COOK TIME 10 MIN.**

Ingredients:
2 tablespoons raw, unfiltered apple cider
2 cups water
1 tablespoon fresh lemon juice
1 teaspoon ground cinnamon
1 teaspoon honey or stevia
1/2 teaspoon grated fresh ginger
Ice cubes
Lemon slices

Nutritional Information (Per Serving):

Calories: 15

Protein: 0g

Carbohydrates: 4g

Sugars: 2g

Fiber: 0.5g

Sodium: 5mg

Potassium: 30mg

Directions:
Measure the apple cider vinegar, water, lemon juice, cinnamon, honey or stevia, and fresh ginger.

In a large glass or pitcher, combine the apple cider vinegar, water, lemon juice, ground cinnamon, honey or stevia, and grated fresh ginger.

Stir the mixture well until the honey (if using) is fully dissolved and all ingredients are evenly distributed.

Let the tonic sit for about 10 minutes to let the flavors meld together.

Serving Suggestions:
Serve this tonic cold as a refreshing drink in the morning or between meals.

Hibiscus Iced Tea

 SERVES 4   **PREP TIME 5 MIN.**   **COOK TIME 10 MIN.**

Ingredients:
4 cups water
1/2 cup dried hibiscus flowers
1-2 tablespoons honey or stevia
1 tablespoon fresh lime juice
1 teaspoon fresh grated ginger
Ice cubes
Lime slices
Fresh mint leaves

Nutritional Information (Per Serving):

Calories: 20

Carbohydrates: 5g

Sugars: 2g

Sodium: 5mg

Potassium: 30mg

Directions:
Bring 4 cups of water to a boil in a medium-sized pot.

Remove the pot from heat and add the dried hibiscus flowers and grated ginger (if using). Stir to combine.

Cover the pot and let the mixture steep for 10-15 minutes to allow the hibiscus and ginger to infuse.

Strain the hibiscus tea into a large pitcher, discarding the solids.

If desired, add honey or stevia to the warm tea and stir until fully dissolved.

Serving Suggestions:
Serve this hibiscus iced tea cold as a refreshing and hydrating beverage.

Beverages for Liver - Cleansing

Herbal Chamomile Tea

 SERVES 4 **PREP TIME** 5 MIN. **COOK TIME** 10 MIN.

Ingredients:
4 cups water
4 tablespoons dried chamomile flowers
,(or 4 chamomile tea bags)
1 tablespoon fresh lemon juice
(optional for added flavor)
1 teaspoon honey or stevia
(optional for sweetness)
1 teaspoon fresh grated ginger
(optional for added flavor and benefits)
Fresh mint leaves (optional, for garnish)

Nutritional Information (Per Serving):
Calories: 5
Carbohydrates: 1g
Sodium: 5mg
Potassium: 10mg

Directions:
Bring 4 cups of water to a boil in a medium-sized pot.
Remove the pot from heat and add the dried chamomile flowers (or tea bags) and grated ginger (if using). Stir to combine.
Cover the pot and let the mixture steep for 5-10 minutes to allow the chamomile and ginger to infuse.
Strain the chamomile tea into a large pitcher or teapot, discarding the solids.
If desired, add honey or stevia to the warm tea and stir until fully dissolved.
Stir in the fresh lemon juice for added flavor and a boost of vitamin C.

Serving Suggestions:
Serve this chamomile tea warm as a soothing and relaxing beverage.

Carrot and Ginger Juice

 SERVES 4 **PREP TIME** 5 MIN. **COOK TIME** 10 MIN.

Ingredients:
4 large carrots
1-inch piece of fresh ginger
1 medium apple
1 tablespoon fresh lemon juice
1 cup water
Ice cubes
Fresh mint leaves

Nutritional Information (Per Serving):
Calories: 60
Protein: 1g
Carbohydrates: 14g
Sugars: 10g
Fiber: 2g
Cholesterol: 0mg
Sodium: 45mg
Potassium: 400mg

Directions:
Peel and chop the carrots and ginger. If using, core and chop the apple. Juice the lemon to obtain fresh lemon juice.
Combine the carrots, ginger, apple (if using), lemon juice, and water in a high-speed blender.
Blend on high until smooth. If the mixture is too thick, add more water to reach the desired consistency.
Pour the juice through a fine-mesh strainer or cheesecloth into a pitcher to remove the pulp if you want a smoother juice. Use a spoon to press the mixture to extract as much juice as possible.

Serving Suggestions:
Serve this juice fresh and cold as a nutritious start to your day or a refreshing mid-day drink.
Pair with a light snack, such as a handful of nuts or a small piece of fruit, for a balanced and liver-friendly treat.

Beverages for Liver - Cleansing

Beetroot and Apple Juice

 SERVES 2   **PREP TIME** 5 MIN.   **COOK TIME** 10 MIN.

Ingredients:
2 medium beetroots
2 medium apples
1 medium carrot
1 tablespoon fresh lemon juice
1-inch piece of fresh ginger
1 cup water
Ice cubes
Fresh mint leaves

Nutritional Information (Per Serving):
Calories: 90
Protein: 1g
Carbohydrates: 22g
Sugars: 18g
Fiber: 3g
Sodium: 70mg
Potassium: 450mg

Directions:
Peel and chop the beetroots, apples, carrot (if using), and ginger. Juice the lemon to obtain fresh lemon juice.
Combine the beetroots, apples, carrot (if using), ginger, lemon juice, and water in a high-speed blender.
Blend on high until smooth. If the mixture is too thick, add more water to reach the desired consistency.
Pour the juice through a fine-mesh strainer or cheesecloth into a pitcher to remove the pulp if you want a smoother juice. Use a spoon to press the mixture to extract as much juice as possible.

Serving Suggestions:
Serve this juice fresh and cold as a nutritious start to your day or a refreshing mid-day drink.

Aloe Vera and Lime Drink

 SERVES 4   **PREP TIME** 5 MIN.   **COOK TIME** 10 MIN.

Ingredients:
1 cup fresh aloe vera gel
2 cups water
2 tablespoons fresh lime juice
1 tablespoon honey or stevia
1 teaspoon grated fresh ginger
Ice cubes
Lime slices
Fresh mint leaves

Nutritional Information (Per Serving):
Calories: 30
Carbohydrates: 8g
Sugars: 5g
Fiber: 1g
Sodium: 10mg
Potassium: 50mg

Directions:
Carefully cut an aloe vera leaf and extract the gel. Measure 1 cup of aloe vera gel.
In a blender, combine the aloe vera gel, water, fresh lime juice, honey or stevia (if using), and grated fresh ginger (if using).
Blend on high until smooth and well combined.
Pour the mixture into a pitcher and refrigerate for at least 30 minutes to allow the flavors to meld and the drink to chill.

Serving Suggestions:
Serve this cold aloe vera and lime drink as a refreshing beverage to start your day or as a hydrating mid-day drink.

Beverages for Liver - Cleansing

Cinnamon and Apple Infused Water

 SERVES 4　 **PREP TIME** 5 MIN.　 **COOK TIME** 10 MIN.

Ingredients:
1 medium apple
2 cinnamon sticks
8 cups water
1 tablespoon fresh lemon juice
Ice cubes
Fresh mint leaves

Nutritional Information (Per Serving):

Calories: 5

Carbohydrates: 1g

Potassium: 10mg

Directions:
Wash and thinly slice the apple. Gather the cinnamon sticks.
Add apple slices and cinnamon sticks in a large pitcher.
Pour 8 cups of water over the apples and cinnamon into the pitcher.
Add the fresh lemon juice to the mixture.
Give the mixture a good stir to combine all the ingredients.
Place the pitcher in the refrigerator and let it chill for 2-4 hours to allow the flavors to infuse.

Serving Suggestions:
Serve this cinnamon and apple-infused water cold as a refreshing and hydrating beverage throughout the day.

Fresh Tomato Juice with Basil

SERVES 2　 **PREP TIME** 5 MIN.　 **COOK TIME** 10 MIN.

Ingredients:
4 medium ripe tomatoes
1/4 cup fresh basil leaves
1 small cucumber
1/4 teaspoon sea salt
1/4 teaspoon black pepper
1 tablespoon fresh lemon juice
1 cup water
Ice cubes
Fresh basil leaves

Nutritional Information (Per Serving):

Calories: 40

Protein: 2g

Carbohydrates: 9g

Sugars: 5g

Fats: 0g

Fiber: 2g

Cholesterol: 0mg

Sodium: 150mg

Potassium: 550mg

Directions:
Wash and chop the tomatoes, basil leaves, and cucumber.
Juice the lemon.
Combine the tomatoes, basil leaves, cucumber, sea salt, black pepper, lemon juice, and water in a high-speed blender.
Blend on high until smooth. If the mixture is too thick, add more water to reach the desired consistency.
Pour the juice through a fine-mesh strainer or cheesecloth into a pitcher to remove any solids for a smoother juice.
Use a spoon to press the mixture to extract as much juice as possible.
If desired, refrigerate the juice for 30 minutes to chill.

Serving Suggestions:
Serve this fresh tomato juice cold as a nutritious start to your day or a refreshing mid-day drink.

Beverages for Liver - Cleansing

Spiced Golden Milk

 **SERVES 2**   **PREP TIME 5 MIN.**   **COOK TIME 15 MIN.**

Ingredients:
2 cups unsweetened almond milk
1 teaspoon ground turmeric
1/2 teaspoon ground cinnamon
1/4 teaspoon ground ginger
1/4 teaspoon ground black pepper
1 teaspoon honey or stevia
1/2 teaspoon vanilla extract
1/2 teaspoon ground cardamom

Nutritional Information (Per Serving):
Calories: 60
Protein: 1g
Carbohydrates: 6g
Sugars: 2g (from honey, if used)
Fats: 3g
Fiber: 1g
Sodium: 150mg
Potassium: 100mg

Directions:
In a small saucepan, heat the almond milk over medium heat until it is warm but not boiling.
Add the ground turmeric, ground cinnamon, ground ginger, and ground black pepper to the milk. Stir well to combine.
If using, add honey or stevia, vanilla extract, and ground cardamom. Stir until everything is well mixed and the honey (if using) is dissolved.
Reduce the heat to low and let the mixture simmer for about 5 minutes, stirring occasionally. Do not let it boil.
Remove the saucepan from the heat and let the golden milk cool slightly for about 5 minutes.

Serving Suggestions:
Serve this spiced golden milk warm as a soothing evening drink or a comforting beverage anytime during the day.

Lemon and Ginger Detox Drink

 SERVES 4   **PREP TIME 5 MIN.**   **COOK TIME 10 MIN.**

Ingredients:
4 cups water
2 tablespoons fresh ginger
1 medium lemon
1 medium lemon
1 teaspoon honey or stevia
Fresh mint leaves
Ice cubes

Nutritional Information (Per Serving):
Calories: 10
Carbohydrates: 2g
Sugars: 1g
Sodium: 5mg
Potassium: 20mg

Directions:
Bring the 4 cups of water to a boil in a medium-sized pot.
Remove the pot from heat and add the thinly sliced fresh ginger. Cover and let it steep for 10 minutes.
Strain the ginger-infused water into a large pitcher, discarding the ginger slices.
Add the fresh lemon juice to the pitcher.
If using, add honey or stevia to the mixture and stir until fully dissolved.
Add the thinly sliced lemon to the pitcher for additional flavor infusion.
Place the pitcher in the refrigerator and let it chill for at least 1 hour to allow the flavors to meld together.

Serving Suggestions:
Serve this lemon and ginger detox drink cold as a refreshing beverage to start your day or as a hydrating drink throughout the day.

Beverages for Liver - Cleansing

Watermelon and Basil Infused Water

 SERVES 4　　 **PREP TIME** 5 MIN.　　 **COOK TIME** 10 MIN.

Ingredients:
4 cups water
2 cups watermelon
1/4 cup fresh basil leaves
1 tablespoon fresh lime juice
Ice cubes

Nutritional Information (Per Serving):

Calories: 10

Carbohydrates: 2g

Sugars: 1g

Potassium: 20mg

Directions:
Wash and cube the watermelon. Wash the fresh basil leaves. Juice the lime if using.
Add watermelon cubes and fresh basil leaves in a large pitcher.
Pour 4 cups of water into the pitcher over the watermelon and basil.
If using, add the fresh lime juice.
Give the mixture a good stir to combine all the ingredients.
Place the pitcher in the refrigerator and let it chill for 1-2 hours to allow the flavors to infuse.

Serving Suggestions:
Serve this watermelon and basil-infused water cold as a refreshing and hydrating beverage throughout the day.

28 DAY MEAL

1 WEEK MEAL PLAN

	BREAKFAST	**LUNCH**	**DINNER**	**SNACKS**
SUN	Avocado Toast with Poached Egg	Lemon Garlic Grilled Tuna with Mixed Greens	Feta, Spinach & Tomato Stuffed Salmon	Cranberry Whipped Feta Dip
MON	Oatmeal with Almonds and Blueberries	Baked Salmon with Asparagus and Cherry Tomatoes	Chicken and Vegetable Rissoles	Pecan Granola Bars
TUE	Veggie Omelet with Spinach and Tomato	Curried Cauliflower and Chickpea Bowl	Sumac Turkey stuffed pittas	Caprese Salad Skewers
WED	Banana and Oat Pancakes	Turkey and Sweet Potato Chilli	Sardine Fish Cakes with Green Mix Salad	Babaganoush
THU	Zucchini Fritters	Grilled Shrimp and Mango Salad	Mackerel with Warm Cauliflower & Caper Salad	Beets with Feta and Pesto sauce
FRI	Sweet Potato and Black Bean Breakfast Burrito	Lentil and Vegetable Stir-Fry	Golden Caulilower Chicken Curry	Tuna and Avocado Tartare
SUN	Cottage Cheese with Pineapple and Flax	Fresh Spring Rolls	Turkey Meatballs in Tomato Sauce	Steamed Edamame

28 DAY MEAL
2 WEEK MEAL PLAN

	BREAKFAST	LUNCH	DINNER	SNACKS
SUN	Hummus and Veggie Breakfast Wrap	Avocado Lime Chicken Salad	Simple Tilapia Skillet	Air Fryer Loaded Zucchini Skins
MON	Healthy shakshuka	Turkey, Strawberry & Avocado Salad	Balsamic Glazed Chicken and Roasted Vegetables	Griled Shrimp with Tzatziki Sauce and Capers
TUE	Blueberry Amond Pancakes	Eggplant and Tomato Stack with Basil	Southwest Turkey Stew	No Bake Blueberry Energy Bites
WED	Baked Apple and Cinnamon Oatmeal	Greek Yogurt Chicken Salad	Baked Chilean Sea Bass	Dip Sause with Artichoke and Kale
THU	Curried broccoli & boiled eggs on toast	Baked Cod with Lemon and Dill	Honey Garlic Chicken Thighs with Carrots and Broccoli	Cucumber Avocado Rolls
FRI	Chia Seed Pudding with Fresh Fruit	Best Buddha Bowl	Mediterranean Turkey Stuffed Peppers	Avocado and Tomato Bruschetta
SUN	Greek Yogurt with Honey and Walnuts	Turkey and Avocado Wrap	Healthy Apricot Chicken	Herby Baked Falafel Bites with Spicy Mint Tahini Dip

28 DAY MEAL
3 WEEK MEAL PLAN

	BREAKFAST	LUNCH	DINNER	SNACKS
SUN	Egg White and Veggie Frittata	Grilled Lemon Herb Chicken Salad	Chargrilled Turkey with Quinoa Tabbouleh & Tahini Dressing	Garden Hummus
MON	Vegan Waffle	Lentil and Vegetable Stir-Fry	Chicken Veloute	Air Fryer Everything Bagel Avocado Fries
TUE	Smoothie Bowl with Fresh Strawberries	Best Buddha Bowl	Chargrilled Mackerel with Sweet & Sour Beetroot	Guacamole with Pita Chips
WED	Omelet with zucchini and herbs	Beet and Goat Cheese Salad Boiled	Cilantro-Lime Shrimps Tacos	Warm Spinach and Artichoke Dip
THU	Buckwheat Pancakes with Maple Syrup and Berries Seeds	Tomato Basil Soup	Chicken & Broccoli Quinoa Casserole	White Bean and Baked Eggplant Hummus
FRI	Banana & Tahini Porridge	Roasted Tomato and Sardine Salad	Salmon En Papillote with Potatoes	Vegan Cauliflower Wings
SUN	Scrambled Tofu with Mushrooms and Peppers	Zucchini Noodles with Pesto and Cherry Tomatoes	Broiled Tilapia with Thai Coconut Curry Sauce	Caprese Salad Skewers

28 DAY MEAL
4 WEEK MEAL PLAN

	BREAKFAST	LUNCH	DINNER	SNACKS
SUN	Persian-Style Spinach & Herb Saute with Eggs	Quinoa and Black Bean Stuffed Bell Peppers	Rolled Turkey Breasts with Herby Lemon & pine nut stuffing	Cranberry Whipped Feta Dip
MON	Quinoa and Berry Bowl	Spinach and Mushrooms Fritata	Moroccan Spiced Fish Stew	Avocado and Tomato Bruschetta
TUE	Chickpea Flour Crepes	Spinach and Feta Stuffed Portobello Mushrooms	Garlicky Lemon Oven Baked Tilapia	Cucumber Avocado Rolls
WED	Avocado Toast with Poached Egg	Grilled Lemon Herb Chicken Salad	Slow Cooker Salmon	Beets with Feta and Pesto sauce
THU	Millet Porridge with Almond Milk and Pears	Broccoli Soup	Easy Honey Garlic Chicken Stir-Fry	Griled Shrimp with Tzatziki Sause and Capers
FRI	Smoothie Bowl with Fresh Strawberries	Baked Salmon with Asparagus and Cherry Tomatoes	Balsamic Glazed Chicken andRoasted Vegetables	Pecan Granola Bars
SUN	Zucchini Fritters	Turkey and Avocado Wrap	Chicken Fried Rice	Beets with Feta and Pesto sauce

MEAL PLANNING TIPS

Practical Advice on Planning and Preparing Meals for Liver Health
Successfully following a fatty liver diet involves more than knowing which foods to eat. It requires practical planning and preparation to ensure that healthy choices are convenient and enjoyable. Here are some tips to help you plan and prepare meals that support liver health:

1. Stock Your Pantry with Liver-Friendly Staples
Having the right ingredients on hand makes it easier to prepare healthy meals. Stock your pantry with these liver-friendly staples:
Whole Grains: Brown rice, quinoa, oats, whole-wheat pasta, and whole-grain bread.
Lean Proteins: Skinless poultry, fish, beans, legumes, and tofu.
Healthy Fats: Olive oil, avocado, nuts, and seeds.
Fruits and Vegetables: Fresh, frozen, or canned (without added sugar or salt) produce.
Herbs and Spices: Basil, cilantro, parsley, turmeric, ginger, garlic, and pepper to add flavor without added salt or sugar.

2. Plan Your Meals Ahead
Planning your meals for the week can help you make healthier choices and reduce stress. Follow these steps:
Weekly Planning: Set aside time each week to plan your meals. Consider breakfast, lunch, dinner, and snacks.
Balanced Meals: Ensure each meal includes a balance of protein, healthy fats, and fiber-rich carbohydrates.
Variety: Include a variety of foods to ensure you get a wide range of nutrients.

3. Make a Grocery List
Based on your meal plan, create a grocery list to ensure you have all the ingredients you need. This can help you avoid impulse purchases and ensure you stick to your healthy eating goals.

4. Prep Ingredients in Advance
Prepping ingredients in advance can save time and make healthy eating more convenient. Here's how:
Chop Vegetables: Wash and chop vegetables for the week, so they're ready to use in recipes or as snacks.
Cook Grains and Proteins: Prepare batches of whole grains and lean proteins, such as grilled chicken or quinoa, to use in various meals.
Portion Snacks: Portion out healthy snacks like nuts, seeds, and fruit to grab and go.

5. Cook in Batches
Cooking in larger quantities can save time and ensure healthy meals are always available. Consider these tips:
Double Recipes: Double the recipes for soups, stews, and casseroles, and freeze the extras for future meals.
Use a Slow Cooker or Instant Pot: These appliances can help you prepare large batches of healthy meals with minimal effort.

6. Pack Your Lunch

Bringing your lunch to work or school can help you control your diet and avoid unhealthy options. Pack balanced meals with lean proteins, whole grains, and plenty of vegetables.

7. Healthy Snack

Keep healthy snacks readily available to avoid reaching for unhealthy options. Some liver-friendly snack ideas include.

8. Stay Hydrated

Hydration is essential for liver health. Drink plenty of water throughout the day and limit sugary drinks and alcohol. Herbal teas and infused water with slices of fruit can be flavorful alternatives.

9. Limit Processed Foods

Processed foods often contain unhealthy fats, sugars, and additives that can harm liver health. Focus on whole, unprocessed foods whenever possible.

10. Listen to Your Body

Pay attention to how different foods make you feel. Everyone's body is different, and adjusting your diet based on your needs and responses is essential.

By incorporating these practical tips into your routine, you can create a sustainable, liver-friendly diet that supports your health and well-being. With a bit of planning and preparation, healthy eating can become an easy and enjoyable part of your daily life.

CONCLUSION

Embarking on a journey to manage or prevent fatty liver disease through diet is empowering and transformative. This cookbook has provided a collection of nutritious, delicious, easy-to-prepare recipes tailored to support liver health. These recipes are designed to nourish your body while promoting liver function and overall well-being by focusing on low-fat, high-fiber, and controlled carbohydrate ingredients.

Throughout these pages, we've explored a variety of meals and beverages that taste great and deliver essential nutrients needed for liver detoxification, inflammation reduction, and overall health improvement. From refreshing detox drinks to hearty meals, each recipe emphasizes the importance of whole, unprocessed foods rich in antioxidants, vitamins, and minerals.

Key takeaways from this cookbook include:

Emphasizing Fresh Ingredients: Fresh fruits, vegetables, and herbs are fundamental to liver health. They provide vital nutrients and antioxidants that help reduce liver inflammation and promote detoxification.

Balancing Macronutrients: A balanced intake of proteins, carbohydrates, and healthy fats supports overall metabolic health and helps maintain a healthy weight, which is crucial for managing fatty liver disease.

Incorporating Anti-inflammatory Foods: Ingredients like turmeric, ginger, garlic, and leafy greens play a significant role in combating inflammation and protecting liver cells from damage.

Hydration and Detoxification: Staying well-hydrated with nutrient-rich beverages such as infused waters, herbal teas, and fresh juices aids in flushing out toxins and keeping the liver functioning optimally.

Mindful Eating: Portion control and mindful eating practices are essential to prevent overeating and manage weight, further reducing the strain on the liver.

As you incorporate these recipes into your daily routine, remember that consistency is critical. Making gradual, sustainable changes to your diet and lifestyle will yield the best results over time. It's not just about a temporary diet; it's about embracing a healthier lifestyle that supports your liver and overall health.

We hope this cookbook has inspired you to take charge of your health and enjoy cooking and eating foods that are both delicious and beneficial for your liver. Here's to a wellness journey filled with flavorful meals and beverages that make every bite and sip a step toward a healthier you.

Thank you for allowing us to be part of your health journey, and we wish you good health and happiness!

Thank you for this purchase!

Your feedback, whether it's a positive rating, a review, or a constructive suggestion, is incredibly valuable. It helps others feel confident about choosing this book and allows us to continue providing great books. You, our awesome customers, are the key to our success.

Share your Amazon experience by SCANNING THE QR CODE
Thank you in advance for your review!

Read Now

You can get your bonus by SCANNING THE QR CODE
50 CHRISTMAS RECIPES

37308199R00066